by Ann Lambert Good

Photos: Courtesy of Steve Good
Website Development: Courtesy of Mike Good

www.mascotbooks.com

St. Louis Cardinals A to Z

Page 88 Sombrero Graphic Vector Graphic by Vecteezy! (www.vecteezy.com)

Project Manager: Kristin Perry
Graphic Designer: Ricky Frame

Busch Stadium Photo: © Brian Gardner
Lou Brock Photo (Brockabrella): © Susan W. Lambert

For more information, please contact:
Mascot Books
560 Herndon Parkway #120
Herndon, VA 20170
info@mascotbooks.com

Library of Congress Control Number: 2017901434

CPSIA Code: PBANG0517A
ISBN-13: 978-1-63177-933-6

Printed in the United States

PREFACE

Welcome to *St. Louis Cardinals A to Z!*

What fun to spend time researching and writing about the Cardinals, especially for a fan; maybe that is why there are so many Cardinals books out there: fun and fandom. So, you think, "why another one?" Well, fans can easily answer that: there is always room for one more! When putting this together I picked topics that interest me; I hope you are interested as well.

ORGANIZATION/INDEX: When you are cruising through, trying to find a particular category, check for it under the letter ("A" for All-Stars) or check the INDEX list in the back. As you can imagine, some letters don't lend themselves easily to the sport, so some creativity was necessary to populate those, especially at the end of the alphabet. So, for instance, look under "Y" ("You're Out") for information on ejections and umpires, and "Z" ("Zeroes") for shutouts and no-hitters. That's where the INDEX might come in handy.

SCOPE: For Cardinals leaders and stat history, some categories include total franchise (since 1892) history, and some the more modern (since 1920) period. The late 1800s guys dominate some stats, so sometimes modern was more interesting.

STATS CHEAT SHEET: For a STATISTICS quick-check on what are good and bad numbers (WAR, WHIP, OPS etc.), check out the STATISTICS appendix in the back of the book.

FUN FACTS: In "FUN FACTS" (after most items), you will find information on the career and single-season MLB leaders (putting Cardinals numbers in context) and some history of baseball.

TOOLS: Thank you to all the amazing research tools on baseball: baseball-reference.com, fangraphs.com, baseball-almanac.com, and the Society for American Baseball Research (SABR).

I hope you enjoy the book!

Ann Lambert Good

INTRODUCTION: ST. LOUIS CARDINALS BALLPARKS

Recalling the Past: "Key Hole Gang" — "Astroturf" — "Cookie Cutter Stadium"

Cardinals ballpark history seemed like a great topic for the book introduction, providing both a context and a launching point for the information in *A to Z*. I have included the locations in case fans want to go visit some of the old spots, and a list of other notable ballparks in St. Louis history (also a map below). The Cardinals ballparks are organized from the first franchise stadium in 1892 to the current one called Busch Stadium III.

SPORTSMAN's PARK 1892

Where was it: Grand and Dodier (See 1920–66 below).

What is there now: The Herbert Hoover Boys & Girls Club, 2901 Grand Avenue.

The St. Louis Browns rejoined the National League after the American Association folded at the end of the season in 1891. Owner Chris Von der Ahe then moved them to a larger facility (New Sportsman's Park/ Robison Field) for 1893 (see next item). Upon arrival from Milwaukee, the American League St. Louis Browns moved into the abandoned park in 1902 and, in 1909, reinforced the structure with concrete and steel. This became the famous Sportsman's Park (see 1920 below) which the Cardinals shared with the Browns (1920–53) and then took over (1953–66) when the Browns departed St. Louis for Baltimore.

ROBISON FIELD 1893–1920

Names: "New Sportsman's Park" (1893–98), "League Park" (1899–1911), "Robison Field" (1911–1917), "Cardinal Field" (1918–1920)

Where was it: Vandeventer & Natural Bridge Avenues, across from Fairgrounds Park. This was the last ballpark made primarily of wood and caught fire a number of times.

What is there now: The ballpark was torn down to build Beaumont High School at 3836 Natural Bridge Avenue in 1925, which closed in May 2014. Earl Weaver, manager of the Orioles, graduated from Beaumont in 1948.

In 1899, the team changed names from the Browns to the Perfectos, and then in 1900 became the Cardinals. Interestingly, New York sportswriters referred to them as "the Terrors" in 1900, possibly due to their 3rd baseman, John McGraw. Owner Von der Ahe had some interesting ideas, and built an amusement park and beer garden next to the ballpark, including a "shoot-the-shoots" water flume ride. Interestingly, the "Knot Hole Gang," a club providing special tickets for kids, originated in St. Louis during this period (1917) as a reward to club investors who put down $50 for a share of stock: one free kid seat in the bleachers. Cardinals president Branch Rickey expanded the kid seat membership idea to include disadvantaged youth and ended up with about 10,000–15,000 kids in the bleacher seats. The term "Knot Hole Gang" started in the days of wooden-fenced ballparks when kids watched games for free through holes in the wood (when the knots popped out).

SPORTMAN'S PARK/BUSCH STADIUM I (1920–1966)

Where was it: Corner of Grand and Dodier, address was 3623 Dodier Street or 2911 N. Grand Boulevard.

What is there today: Site of the Herbert Hoover Boys & Girls Club, 2901 N. Grand Avenue.

1920–1952: Sportsman's Park (Shared by the Cardinals and Browns)

The Cardinals sold Robison Field and moved into Sportsman's Park in 1920, becoming tenants of the American League Browns; they played their first game there on July 1, 1920. Proceeds from the sale of Cardinal Park were invested in the first farm club affiliation in Houston, Texas. The Cardinals finally got to the World Series in 1926, winning six championships during this phase (1926, 1931, 1934, 1942, 1944, 1946). The 1944 World Series featured Cardinals vs. Browns in only the 3rd series played entirely in one stadium (Cardinals won 4–2). The Browns did not have much success on the field, but owner Bill Veeck put on some flashy promotions, including the famous Eddie Gaedel appearance in 1951 as the shortest (3 feet 7 inches) batter, wearing jersey number 1/8, in Major League history. Gaedel made his entrance popping out of a large "birthday cake." Five days later, Veeck held "Grandstand Manager's Day," letting fans vote on some in-game strategy decisions (bunt, steal, change pitchers); straight-laced Connie Mack and the Athletics were on the other side. The Browns won!

1953–1966: Busch Stadium (Sportsman's Park refurbished)

Sportsman's Park was purchased and renamed after Anheuser-Busch, Inc. bought the Cardinals in 1953. There was originally a plan to name the stadium "Budweiser" after the beer, but Baseball Commissioner Ford Frick vetoed the name for "public relations" reasons. The new owner

spent $1.5 million on renovations during 1953–54, removed extraneous advertising, and put up the neon eagle on top of the scoreboard in right field which flapped its wings for every Cardinals home run (see "E" for eagle in the book). In 1955, management decided to remove the "temporary" screen in right field (put up by the Browns in 1929 to reduce opposition home runs) to help the slugging Cardinals. It did not work well (still opposition friendly), so the screen went back up the next year and remained until the end. The last game was played on May 8, 1966. In a closing ceremony that day, a helicopter transported home plate to the site of the new Busch Stadium II. During these years, the Cardinals had one World Series Championship in 1964.

BUSCH STADIUM II STADIUM (1966–2005)

Where was it: Located at Stadium Plaza, Spruce and Walnut, about where Ballpark Village is now.

What is there now: Busch Stadium III and Ballpark Village.

The official name was Civic Center Busch Memorial Stadium, and it was completed after the St. Louis Arch went up in 1965, making a dramatic skyline along with the 96 arches cut out circling the top of the stadium. Opening day ceremonies on May 12, 1966 included a helicopter delivering the American flag. Concessions that day featured ham and cheese sandwiches because the gas grills for hot dogs had not yet been hooked up. The multipurpose stadium featured Astroturf from 1970–1995 in order to make the transition from football to baseball easier, resulting in an even hotter stadium in the summer (the Blue Jays and Rays are the only MLB teams left on artificial turf). It was the last of the "cookie cutter"-style stadiums of the 1960s and 1970s to close. The Cardinals played in a total of six World Series, winning two Championships in 1967 and 1982 (losses in 1968, 1986, 1987, and 2004).

BUSCH STADIUM III (2006–present)

Where is it: 700 Clark Street; occupies a portion of the Busch Stadium II footprint.

The Cardinals became the first team since the 1923 Yankees to win a World Series Championship in the inaugural season of a new ballpark (Yankees did it again in 2009), and won a second championship in 2011. The first game was on April 10, 2006 against the Brewers, a 6–4 win. 2005 Cy Young winner Chris Carpenter and 2005 National League MVP Albert Pujols threw out first pitches to two-time Cy Young winner Bob Gibson (Carpenter) and 1985 National League MVP Willie McGee (Pujols). In 2016, there were 10th anniversary celebrations with "Base Burglar" Lou Brock (Loooooou!) throwing out the first pitch.

OTHER BALLPARKS IN ST. LOUIS HISTORY

Red Stockings Park (1874–1898) aka Compton Park: South Compton Avenue and Gratiot Street. Home of the St. Louis Red Stockings of the National Association, this was reportedly the location of the first professional baseball game in St. Louis on May 4, 1875. The facility was torn down in 1898.

Union Base Ball Park (1884–late 1880s) aka Lucas Park: Northeast corner of Cass and Jefferson Avenues, home of the St. Louis Maroons of the Union Association (1884) and the National league (1885–86). The park seated 10,000 and had a scoreboard where scores from around the league (sent by telegraph) were posted. The Maroons big star was pitcher Charlie Sweeney; the team relocated in 1887 to become the Indianapolis Hoosiers.

Giants Park (1907–1921) aka Kuebler's Park: North Broadway Avenue and Clarence. This park was home to a Negro League team called the St. Louis Giants in the early 1900s, which became the St. Louis Stars (see below).

Federal League Park (1914–1915) aka Handlan's Park: NE corner of Grand and Laclede. The park was home of the St. Louis Terriers during the two years of the short-lived Federal League. HOF pitchers Mordecai Brown and Eddie Plank played for the Terriers. Today, Wrigley Field (Cubs) is the only Federal League ballpark still standing (then called Weeghman Park, opened in 1914). After the Federal League shut down, the park was used as the St. Louis University Athletic Field.

Stars Park (1922–33): SE corner of Compton and North Market—now occupied by Harris-Stowe State College. Stars Park was built specifically for the St. Louis All-Stars, the team where the legendary "Cool Papa" Bell got his start; another HOFer, Oscar Charleston, played there as well. The team won Negro National League titles in 1928 and 1930.

MAP OF THE BALLPARKS:

This map is from an article entitled "The Bygone Ballparks of St. Louis" by Cameron Collins (Apr 1, 2013), posted on distilledhistory.com. This article provided good information which was also based on a book, *St. Louis' Big League Ballparks,* by Joan M. Thomas.

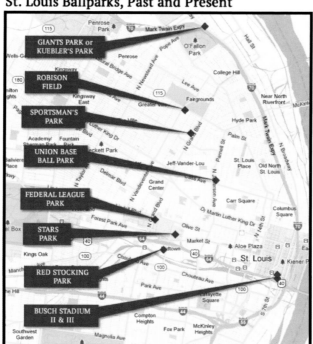

St. Louis Ballparks, Past and Present

is for...

ALL-STAR CARDINALS

#1	**Stan Musial OF/1B**	**24**
#2	Ozzie Smith SS	14
#3	Ken Boyer 3B	11
#4	Enos Slaughter RF	10
#5	Red Schoendienst 2B	9
	Bob Gibson RHP	9
#6	Albert Pujols 1B	9
#7	Marty Marion SS	8
#8	Yadier Molina C	7
#9	Lou Brock LF	6
	Joe Medwick LF	6
	Ted Simmons C	6

FUN FACT: In 2016, the Cubs' whole infield was elected to start the All-Star game, the first time in the NL since the 1963 Cardinals dominated the infield starting lineup: Bill White (1B), Julian Javier (2B), Ken Boyer (3B), and Dick Groat (SS).

All-Star CARDINALS:
First All-Star Game in 1933 *(Four Starters)*

*July 6, 1933 at Comiskey Park, home of the Chicago White Sox

*Players selected by managers and fans

*National League lost 4–2

- **Bill Hallahan (P):** Starting pitcher vs. AL Lefty Gomez; 2 IP/gave up 3 earned runs

- **Jimmie Wilson (C):** went 0–4

- **Frankie Frisch (2B):** 2-out solo HR in the 6th off General Crowder

- **Pepper Martin (3B):** 1 RBI, scoring Lon Warneke

HOFers: Frankie Frisch, Bill Terry, Chick Hafey, Chuck Klein, Lefty Gomez, Rick Ferrell, Lou Gehrig, Charlie Gehringer, Joe Cronin, Al Simmons, Babe Ruth, AL Manager Connie Mack, and NL Manager John McGraw.

FUN FACT – *Addie Joss All-Star Game (1911):* The first unofficial "All-Star" game took place on July 24, 1911, featuring the American League all-stars against the Cleveland Naps in a fundraiser to benefit the family of pitching great Addie Joss (HOF 1978), who passed away suddenly in his prime at age 31. The game featured a number of HOFers, including Eddie Collins, Tris Speaker, Walter Johnson, Napoleon

Lajoie, Gabby Street, Sam Crawford, Smokey Joe Wood, Frank "Home Run" Baker, and Ty Cobb (who wore a Cleveland uniform because he lost his on the way). A panoramic photo of the event sold in 2005 for almost $90,000. In it, player Jack Graney managed to be in the photo twice doing a "pizza run" from being 3 in on the left to being the last one on the right. A different style of photo bombing. The impromptu benefit raised about $300,000 (today's money) for the Joss family.

All-Star CARDINALS:
MLB Records Held by CARDINALS

Record	Player	Statistic
Games Played	Stan Musial	24 (tied with Willie Mays and Hank Aaron)
Extra Base Hits	Stan Musial	8 (tied with Willie Mays)
Home Runs	Stan Musial	6
Total Bases	Stan Musial	40 (tied with Willie Mays)
Pinch Hits	Stan Musial	3

*Musial All-Star starts: 4 at 1B (1950, 1957, 1958, 1959), 5 at LF (1943, 1946, 1948, 1951, 1953), 3 at RF (1944, 1949, 1952).

*Musial All-Star games: 1943–1944, 1946–63 (appeared in 2 All-Star games in 1959–62).

*Musial career All-Star stats: .317/.394/.635 (BA/OBP/SLG)

FUN FACT: In addition to the above, Stan Musial is #2 all-time in: Plate Appearances (PA) with 72 (tied with Hank Aaron), Runs Scored (R) with 11, Hits (H) with 20, and Runs Batted In (RBI) with 10 (tied with Fred Lynn). As noted above, Musial appeared in 2 All-Star games several years when MLB held 2 games in 2 different cities on 2 different dates, reportedly as a way of boosting the players' pension funds.

All-Star CARDINALS:
#2 Most All-Stars in MLB History

#1 Yankees	418
#2 Cardinals	314
#3 Red Sox	289
#4 Dodgers	287
#5 Reds	264

FUN FACT: The team with the most players starting an All-Star Game is the Yankees in 1939 with 6 starting players: Red Rolfe (3B), Joe DiMaggio (CF), Bill Dickey (C), George Selkirk, (LF) Joe Gordon (2B), and Red Ruffing (P). In 1957, the Reds "stuffed" the ballot box and elected 7, but the commissioner stepped in and adjusted the total, replacing 2 Reds with other teams' players. The Cubs have had 216 All-Stars.

ALL-STAR GAMES IN ST. LOUIS

(**BROWNS HOSTED GAME)

July 9, 1940 at Sportsman's Park

Host: St. Louis Cardinals

National League won 4–0

Managers: Joe Cronin (Boston/AL) and Bill McKechnie (Reds/NL)

Starting Pitchers: Red Ruffing (Yankees), Paul Derringer (Reds)

Winning pitcher: Paul Derringer (Yankees)

Attendance: 32, 373

Notable: First All-Star game ending in a shutout; holds record as shortest 9-inning All-Star game: 1 hour, 53 minutes. Hero of the game: Max West (Boston Braves OF), with a home run in the 1st. Cardinals: Johnny Mize (1B), Terry Moore (OF).

Radio Announcers: Red Barber and Bob Elson (Mutual), Mel Allen and France Laux (CBS), Gabby Street (KXOK)

**July 13, 1948 at Sportsman's Park

Host: St. Louis Browns

American League won 5–2

Managers: Bucky Harris (Yankees) and Leo Durocher (Dodgers)

Starting Pitchers: Walt Masterson (Senators) and Ralph Branca (Browns)

Winning Pitcher: Vic Raschi (Yankees)

Attendance: 34,009

Notable: Stan Musial (CARDS) Total bases – 5, home runs – 1, RBI – 2. Cardinals: Musial (OF), Red Schoendienst (2B), Enos Slaughter (OF), Marty Marion (replaced–injury), Harry Brecheen (P–did not pitch).

Radio Announcers: Mel Allen, Jim Britt, and France Laux (Mutual)

July 9, 1957 at Busch Stadium I

Host: St. Louis Cardinals

American League won 6–5

Managers: Casey Stengel (Yankees) and Walter Alston (Dodgers)

Starting Pitchers: Jim Bunning (Tigers) and Curt Simmons (Phillies)

Winning Pitcher: Jim Bunning (Tigers)

Attendance: 30,693

Notable: Controversy over the Reds stuffing the ballot boxes, electing almost the entire team (the commissioner adjusted the numbers). Cardinals: Stan Musial (1B), Wally Moon (OF), Larry Jackson (P), Hal Smith (C–did not play).

Radio Announcers: Bob Neal and Harry Caray (NBC)

TV Announcers: Mel Allen and Al Helfer (NBC)

July 12, 1966 at Busch Stadium II

Host: St. Louis Cardinals

National League won 2–1

Managers: Sam Mele (Twins) and Walter Alston (Dodgers)

Starting Pitchers: Denny McLain (Tigers) and Sandy Koufax (Dodgers)

Winning Pitcher: Gaylord Perry

Attendance: 49,936

Notable: Weather was a hot and humid 105 degrees thru 10 innings; Vice President Hubert Humphrey threw out the first pitch; McLain pitched 3 perfect innings. Cardinals: Curt Flood (OF), Tim McCarver (C), Bob Gibson (P).

TV Announcers: Curt Gowdy and Pee Wee Reese (NBC)

MVP: Brooks Robinson 3B Orioles (on the losing side but played all 10 innings)

July 14, 2009 at Busch Stadium III

Host: St. Louis Cardinals

American League won 4–3

Managers: Joe Maddon (TB Rays) and Charlie Manuel (Phillies)

Starting Pitchers: Roy Halladay (Blue Jays) and Tim Lincecum (Giants)

Winner Pitcher: Jonathan Papelbon (Red Sox)

Attendance: 46,760

Notable: Shortest game since 1988 at 2 hours, 31 minutes; AL retired 18 straight batters, the second most in All-Star game history. President Barack Obama threw out first pitch. Cardinals: Yadier Molina (C), Albert Pujols (1B), Ryan Franklin (P).

TV Announcers: Joe Buck and Tim McCarver (Fox)

MVP: Carl Crawford OF TB Rays

FUN FACT: What about the Home Run Derby? No Cardinal has ever won the Home Run Derby, which started in 1985. Cardinals participants included: Jack Clark (1985), Ray Lankford (1997), Mark McGwire (1998 & 99), Jim Edmonds (2003), Albert Pujols (2003, 2007, 2009), Matt Holliday (2010 & 2011), and Carlos Beltran (2012).

AT BATS (AB) AND PLATE APPEARANCES (PA)

Plate Appearance (PA): Every time a batter completes a turn at bat.

At Bat (AB): PA resulting in a hit, fielder's choice, strikeout, batted out, or reaching base on an error. NO AB for: walk, sacrifice hit, hit by pitch, or catcher's interference.

PA Single-Season (AB): Top 5

Rank	Plate Appearances	At Bats	Player	Year
1	752	648	Taylor Douthit (OF)	1928 (#20 in MLB)
2	748	664	Taylor Douthit (OF)	1930
3	739	679	Curt Flood (OF)	1964
4	729	664	Lou Brock (OF)	1970
5	728	650	Don Blasingame (2B)	1957

AB Single-Season (PA): Top 5

#1	**689** (724)	Lou Brock (1967) (#20 in MLB)
#2	679 (739)	Curt Flood (1964)
#3	672 (696)	Garry Templeton (1979)
#4	664 (729)	Lou Brock (1970)
	664 (748)	Taylor Douthit (1930)
#5	662 (714)	Curt Flood (1963)

FUN FACT: Stan Musial is the #1 Cardinal for career PA/AB (12,712/10,972). Pete Rose holds the MLB record for career PA/AB with 15,861/14,053. The #1 in single-season PA/AB in MLB is Jimmy Rollins (Phillies SS) with 778/716 in 2007. The Cardinal who has the record for the most times facing a pitcher with no official at bats is Miller Huggins with 6 on June 1, 1910; he had 4 walks, 1 sacrifice hit, and 1 sacrifice fly.

ATTENDANCE Records

Attendance: Highest Attendance at Home Games (all at Busch Stadium II)

#1: 53,415—Sat, July 30, 1994   vs. Cubs (W 10–7)

Starting Lineup: Bernard Gilkey (LF), Ozzie Smith (SS), Gregg Jefferies (1B), Ray Lankford (CF), Todd Zeile (3B), Mark Whiten (RF), Geronimo Pena (2B), Tom Pagnozzi (C), Bob Tewksbury (P). WP: Tewksbury. LP: Willie Banks. Save: René Arocha.

#2: 53,146—Sat, July 10, 1993   vs. Rockies (W 9–3)

Starting Lineup: Luis Alicea (2B), Ozzie Smith (SS), Gregg Jefferies (1B), Todd Zeile (3B), Bernard Gilkey (LF), Brian Jordan (CF), Mark Whiten (RF), Tom Pagnozzi (C), Donovan Osborne (P). WP: Osborne. LP: Butch Henry.

#3: 52,876—Sat, Sep 28, 1996   vs. Reds (W 5–2)

Starting Lineup: Ozzie Smith (SS), Willie McGee (CF), Ron Gant (LF), Brian Jordan (RF), Gary Gaetti (3B), John Mabry (1B), Danny Sheaffer (C), Luis Alicea (2B), Danny Jackson (P). WP: Danny Jackson. LP: Mike Morgan. Save: Rick Honeycutt.

FUN FACT: The largest attendance at Busch Stadium III (2006–present) was on opening day—April 13, 2015 vs. Milwaukee: 47,875. Brewers won 5–4, WP Matt Garza, LP Adam Wainwright, SV Francisco Rodriguez.

ATTENDANCE:
Top 3 CARDINALS Seasons

Rank	Year	Total Attendance	Stadium
1	2007	3,552,180	Busch Stadium III (record 78–84) 3rd/NL Central
2	2014	3,540,649	Busch Stadium III (record 90–72) Lost NLCS 4–1
3	2005	3,538,988	Busch Stadium II (record 100–62) Lost NLCS 4–2

ATTENDANCE:
Best Year at Each Stadium

Robison Field (1893–1920): 1911

447,768   75–74 record   Mgr: Roger Bresnahan

Sportsman's Park (1920–1952): 1949

| 1,430,676 | 96–58 record | Mgr: Eddie Dyer |

Busch Stadium I (1953–1966): 1965

| 1,241,201 | 80–81 record | Mgr: Red Schoendienst |

Busch Stadium II (1966–2005): 2005

| 3,538,988 | 100–62 record | Mgr: Tony La Russa |

Busch Stadium III (2006–today): 2007

| 3,552,180 | 83–78 record | Mgr: Tony La Russa |

FUN FACT: The largest attendance in MLB history was 115,301 at a pre-season game between the defending champ Red Sox and the Dodgers on Saturday, March 29, 2008 at the Los Angeles Coliseum. The smallest attendance was 0 (zero!) at the Orioles–White Sox game at Camden Yards on April 29, 2015 following the Baltimore protests; the game was closed to spectators for safety reasons.

is for...

BATTING AVERAGE (BA)

#1	**.359**	Rogers Hornsby 2B (#2 overall MLB)
#2	.336	Johnny Mize 1B
#3	.335	Joe Medwick LF
#4	.331	Stan Musial OF
#5	.328	Albert Pujols 1B
#6	.326	Chick Hafey OF
#7	.325	Jim Bottomley 1B
#8	.312	Frankie Frisch 2B
#9	.308	Joe Torre 1B/C
#10	.307	Ripper Collins 1B

FUN FACT: Cardinals BA leader Hornsby is 2nd to Ty Cobb (Tigers) with .367. Interestingly, 8 of the top 10 in career BA are left-handed batters, only 2 are right-handed (Hornsby and Ed Delahanty of the Phillies), according to baseball-reference.com. The lefties include Ted Williams (Red Sox), Babe Ruth (Yankees), Shoeless Joe Jackson (White Sox), and Tris Speaker (Red Sox/Indians).

BA: Single-Season Leaders

Rank	Batting Avg.	Player	Year
1	.424	Rogers Hornsby (2B)	1924 (#1 overall in MLB since 1900)
2	.403	Rogers Hornsby (2B)	1925
3	.401	Rogers Hornsby (2B)	1922
4	.397	Rogers Hornsby (2B)	1921
5	.396	Jesse Burkett (LF)	1899
6	.384	Rogers Hornsby (2B)	1923
7	.376	Stan Musial (OF)	1948
8	.376	Jesse Burkett (LF)	1901
9	.374	Joe Medwick (OF)	1937
10	.371	Jim Bottomley (1B)	1925

FUN FACT: Rogers Hornsby won 6 consecutive batting titles from 1920–25, averaging .402 in the last 5 of those seasons.

★ ★ ★ BATTING ★ ★ ★
LEADERS

BABIP (Batting Average on Balls in Play)

Measures how often a ball in play goes for a hit.

BABIP: Pitchers Top 5 Single-Season
(minimum 240 IP – since 1920)

#1	Bill Sherdel LHP	.309	1922
#2	Adam Wainwright RHP	.305	2013
#3	Larry Jackson RHP	.302	1959
#4	Bob Gibson RHP	.299	1970
	Dizzy Dean RHP	.299	1932
#5	Bill Hallahan LHP	.298	1931

FUN FACT: Rollie Naylor (Athletics) is the #1 pitcher in single-season MLB for BABIP (minimum 240 IP since 1920) with .337 in 1920. Randy Johnson (Diamondbacks) is #2 with 3.26 in 2000.

BABIP: Batters Top 5 Single-Season
(since 1920)

#1	Rogers Hornsby	.422	1924 (#3 in MLB)
#2	Rogers Hornsby	.409	1921
#3	Willie McGee	.399	1990
#4	Willie McGee	.395	1985
	Jim Bottomley	.395	1923
#5	Rogers Hornsby	.394	1930

FUN FACT: Since 1920, Babe Ruth (Yankees) is #1 in MLB for BABIP with .423 in 1923, George Sisler (Browns) is #2 with .422 in 1922, and Hornsby (above) is #3 with .422 in 1924.

BIRDS ON THE BAT
LOGO – HISTORY

Red: In the first 2 decades of the 1900s, the team was known as the Cardinals because of the brilliant "cardinal" red trim on their uniforms.

Birds: Branch Rickey, then Cardinals VP and GM, was inspired to use the cardinal bird on a bat during a visit to a Men's Fellowship Club meeting at the Ferguson Presbyterian Church where he was the featured speaker on February 16, 1921. The red cardinal birds were table decorations created by congregant Alli May Schmidt.

Rickey tasked Allie May's father, Edward H. Schmidt (head of the art department at the Woodward and Tiernan Printing Co.), to create a logo for the Cardinals' uniforms.

Logo: Since 1922, the May/Schmidt-inspired two "birds on the bat" logo has graced the Redbird uniforms. The logo made its debut in the home opener vs. the Pirates on April 12, 1922. The new logo was pretty colorful for the time with the black bat and red birds, and the beginning Cardinals letter "C" hooked around the bat. St. Louis Post-Dispatch columnist L.C. Davis composed an opening day poem:

> The Cardinals' new uniform
> Will take the populace by storm---
> For they are sure a classy bunch of dressers.
> They'll set the pace, likewise the style,
> And win the pennant by a mile
> Unless the local fans are rotten guessers.

Current Birds: The current "bird on the bat" logo, with a yellow bat, was introduced in 1998.

BUSCH STADIUM III FIRSTS

First Baseball Game: April 4, 2006 between St. Louis Cardinals Minor League affiliates, the Springfield Cardinals and the Memphis Redbirds.

Inaugural MLB Game: April 10, 2006, Cards–6, Brewers–4. Attendance: 41,936. Starting Pitchers: Mark Mulder (Cards) and Tomo Ohka (Brewers). Managers: Tony La Russa (Cards) and Ned Yost (Brewers).

Ceremonial First Pitches at Inaugural Game: Chris Carpenter (P) and Albert Pujols (1B) (winners of the 2005 NL Cy Young and MVP awards), to Cardinals alumni Bob Gibson (P) and Willie McGee (OF).

First Cardinals Hit: David Eckstein, 2nd inning, April 10, 2006

First Cardinals Home Run: Albert Pujols, 3rd inning, April 10, 2006

First Cardinals Win: Mark Mulder, April 10, 2006

First World Series Championship:
vs. Tigers 2006

BROADCASTS: RADIO AND T.V.

RADIO: First Cardinals Broadcast 1926

The first broadcast took place during the 1926 World Series (the Cardinals first), and featured play-by-play man Graham McNamee using a hookup at WEAF and broadcast in St Louis on KSD. He was named the 2016 Ford C. Frick Award recipient for "major contributions to the game of baseball" and is considered the first color commentator.

RADIO: First Cardinals Regular Season Broadcasts 1927 on KMOX

In 1927, owner Sam Breadon gave permission for Cards home games to be broadcast on KMOX with local announcer Garnett Marks. Born in St. Louis in 1899, Marks broadcast every home game in 1927 and 1928, and when the Cards weren't playing (rainouts and open days), he would broadcast the most important out-of-town game using play-by-play accounts furnished by the ticker.

RADIO: First Cardinals Full-Time Radio Announcer France Laux

France Laux became the first full-time radio voice of the Cardinals beginning in 1929 for KMOX. He was also the voice for the St. Louis Browns; the Cards and Browns shared Sportsman's Park and rarely played on the same day. He continued for both teams until 1942, and then worked solely for the Cards in 1943. Laux was hugely popular in St. Louis, and won the first Sporting News Announcer of the Year award in 1937.

RADIO: KMOX

The inaugural broadcast of KMOX took place on Christmas Eve in 1925, with the original two towers located in a pasture on Geyer Road north of Manchester in Kirkwood. KMOX was licensed as the "Voice of St. Louis," and legend has it the KMOX stands for "Kirkwood Missouri, on Xmas." According to KMOX, the call letters were assigned by the Federal Radio Commission; "K" was the assigned first call letter for all new radio stations west of the Mississippi River at that time.

FUN FACT: The first MLB game broadcast on radio was on August 5, 1921 on KDKA of Pittsburgh; the Pirates defeated the Phillies 8–5. The announcer was KDKA staff announcer Harold Arlin. KDKA was the first commercially licensed radio station in the US.

T.V.: First Cardinals Broadcasters in 1947

Harry Caray and Gabby Street were the first Cardinals announcers in 1947 on KSD-TV (carried on radio as well). KSD was the 7th television station to sign on in the US, and the 1st station in Missouri. KSD broadcast the Cards from 1949–87 and 1948–2006.

BROADCASTERS: Jack Buck (1954–59, 1961–2001)

Awards: Recognized by the Baseball Hall of Fame (HOF) with the Ford C. Frick Award in 1987. He was also inducted into the Broadcasters Hall of Fame, the Radio Hall of Fame, and the St. Louis Cardinals Hall of Fame. Buck received a Purple Heart for his service in World War II.

Baseball Start: Buck got his start broadcasting games for the Cardinals with the Columbus Red Birds Triple-A team (1950–51) after successfully auditioning for GM Al Banister. For the audition, he recreated an entire baseball game from a play-by-play account in "The Sporting News." He moved on to the Rochester Red Wings during 1953, which was managed by Bing Devine who recommended Buck to the big club which had just been bought by Anheuser Busch. After another audition, and what seemed like a long wait, he was hired in 1954 as the color man to team up with Harry Caray, the play-by-play

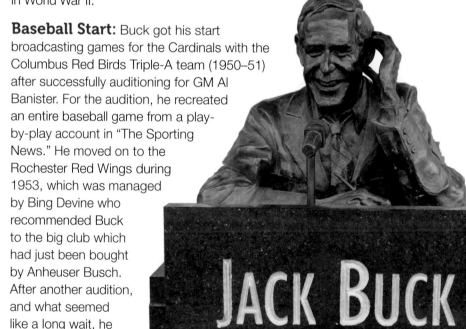

JACK BUCK

JACK BUCK
August 21, 1924 - June 18, 2002

This statue, unveiled August 30, 1998, features Jack in his favorite spot...behind the microphone. "The Voice of the Cardinals" broadcasted more than 8,500 games. Member of 11 Halls of Fame including baseball, football, and radio. One of the all-time greats, he was St. Louis' top Master of Ceremonies and was known for his great sense of humor and charitable work. "The Voice of Summer", Jack was the ticket to the game for those who could not be here... Go Crazy, Folks... That's a Winner!

announcer, and Milo Hamilton, for the broadcasts on KMOX. All three of those 1954 announcers have plaques in the Hall of Fame (HOF).

Career: In addition to the games, Buck did a nightly show from Stan Musial & Biggies Restaurant playing music and doing interviews. Former Cardinals catcher Joe Garagiola joined the team in 1955 and after Caray's departure in 1969, Buck became the lead play-by-play man. The year 1972 saw the arrival of former Cardinals OF Mike Shannon, Buck's partner for the rest of his career, and where he remains to this day. Buck is the longest-serving Cardinal announcer in club history.

BROADCASTERS: Mike Shannon (1972–present)

Awards: St. Louis Cardinals Hall of Fame (2014), local Emmy Award (1985), Missouri Sportscaster of the Year (2002, 2003); two-time World Series champion as a Cardinal player (1964 and 1967).

Baseball: Raised in St. Louis, Shannon made his debut for the Cardinals on September 11, 1962 and played OF until 1967 when he shifted to 3B. Shannon became a hometown hero, hitting a dramatic game-tying home run (hitting the "U" on the Budweiser sign atop the 75-foot-high scoreboard) off of Yankee pitcher Whitey Ford in game 1 of the 1964 World Series. He was forced to leave baseball early in 1970 for health reasons, but made a successful transition to a broadcasting career.

Career: Shannon stayed with the Cardinals in 1971, serving in the front office doing promotions and sales, and after turning down General Manager Bing Devine's offers for coaching/managing positions in 1972 for family and financial reasons, he accepted the job to do color commentary working with a great mentor, Jack Buck, working together 30 years until Buck's retirement. Since that time, Shannon has become an institution well-known for his "Shannon-isms" (see "Q"– quotes), and is likely the longest-serving Cardinals careerist with more than 50 years working with the club. In his spare time, he opened several restaurants, Mike Shannon's Grill, currently located in Edwardsville, Illinois, and Lambert Airport.

BROADCASTERS: NOTABLE CARDINALS PERSONALITIES

Jack Buck (1954–59, 1961–2001):
Ford C. Frick Award (HOF) 1987

Joe Buck (1991–2007):
Jack's son, Fox Sports NFL/MLB/PGA

Harry Caray (1945–69):
Ford C. Frick Award (HOF) 1989

Bob Carpenter (1984, 1995–2001):
currently with the Nationals

Dizzy Dean (1941–46):
former Cardinals P (HOF)

Jim Edmonds (2013–present):
former Cardinals CF 2000–07, Cardinals HOF

Joe Garagiola (1955–62):
St. Louis native, former Cardinals C 1946–51

Jerry Gross (1961, 1963–67):
later with the Padres, Indiana Pacers

Rick Horton (2008–present):
former Cardinals P 1984–87

Al Hrabosky (1985–present):
former Cardinals P, NL saves leader 1975

France Laux (1929–43, 1945):
called Browns weekend games until 1953

Tim McCarver (2014–present):

former Cardinals C, 2012 Ford C. Frick Award (HOF)

Dan McLaughlin (1999–present):

St. Louis native, also worked Mizzou Tiger games

Jay Randolph (1973–87, 2007–10):

also did the first season of St. Louis Blues Hockey

John Rooney (2006–present):

a Missouri native, also called Mizzou Tigers Basketball

Mike Shannon (1972–present):

former Cardinals OF 1962–70, Cardinals HOF

Gabby Street (1945–50):

Cardinals Manager 1929, 1930–33; World Series 1931

FUN FACT: The first MLB game T.V. broadcast was on August 26, 1939 on station W2XBS (later WNBC-TV), with announcer Red Barber calling Dodgers–Reds game at Ebbets Field in Brooklyn, New York (Dodgers–6, Reds–1). The first national T.V. broadcast was on October 1, 1951 on NBC: the Dodgers beat the Giants in the first game of a playoff series by 3–1 on Bobby Thomson's 3-run game-winning home run (Thomson's "Shot Heard Around the World" off of Ralph Branca happened later in the 3rd game).

CARDS—CUBS RIVALRY:

BIRDS ON THE BAT VS. BOYS IN BLUE

CARDS—CUBS Rivalry: New Chapter NLDS 2015

The Cards and Cubs met for the first time ever in the postseason in the National League Division Series (NLDS) in 2015. The Cubs beat the Pirates 4–0 in the wild card game to advance to the NLDS versus the Cards. The Cubs won the NLDS 3–1:

- Cards won Game 1 at home (4–0); WP–John Lackey (Cubs LP–Jon Lester).

- Cubs won Game 2 (Busch), a 6–3 loss, with three solo home runs by Matt Carpenter (IF), Kolten Wong (2B), and Randal Grichuk (OF).

- Cubs set a new MLB playoff record with 6 home runs by 6 different players in their Game 3 victory at home (13–8).

- Cubs won the series in Game 4 (6–4) at Wrigley.

- Cubs moved on, and were swept by the Mets (4–0) in the National League Conference Series (NLCS).

CARDS–CUBS Rivalry: Numbers

- Cards biggest win over the Cubs: 20–5 on April 16, 1912

- 311 players "shared:" including Harry Caray, Jason Heyward, and John Lackey

- World Series Championships: Cards 11, Cubs 3 (1907, 1908, 2016)

- National League (NL) Pennants: Cards 19, Cubs 17

- National League (NL) Batting Titles: Cards 22, Cubs 7

- National League (NL) ERA Leader: Cards 12, Cubs 10

- Rookies of the Year (ROY): Cards 6, Cubs 5

- MVPs: Cards 20, Cubs 10

- Gold Glove Awards: Cards 88, Cubs 37

- Hall of Famers: Cards 17, Cubs 14

- Wins: Cubs lead with 1,207 to 1,156 (19 ties) through 2016

- Postseason: 1 post-season play-off series (see above) in the 2015 National League Division Series (Cubs won 3-1)

- Famous Trade: "Brock-for-Broglio Trade" in 1964

- Home Run Chase 1998: Mark McGwire 70 vs. Sammy Sosa 66

- Radio & Overlapping Fan Territory: KMOX vs. WGN (both huge)

- Cy Young Winners: Cardinals 3, Cubs 5

- Managers of the Year: Cardinals 2, Cubs 4

FUN FACT: It's historic and fun; one of the great rivalries in MLB. The Cubs were a more dominant team in the first part of the 1900s. Things heated up in 1945 when the Cubs won the pennant, beating the Cardinals by three games. In other developments, Cubs pitcher Don Cardwell threw a no-hitter against the Cardinals on June 15, 1964. The Brock-for-Broglio trade, which became a symbol for a lopsided trade, aggravated things on the Cubs' (losing) side in June, 1964. On September 22, 1974, bad feelings were exchanged over a delayed at-bat, resulting in Cardinals catcher Ted Simmons decking Cubs pitcher Bill Madlock.

CY YOUNG AWARDS *(THREE)*

1968: Bob Gibson RHP (33 years old): 22–9, ERA 1.12, 268 Strikeouts

Posted 1.12 ERA, the lowest since Dutch Leonard (0.96) in 1914, with 13 shutouts

Won all 12 starts in June/July, all complete games including 8 shutouts

Finished with 28 complete games out of 34 and, of those 6 not complete, he was removed for a pinch hit, not for another pitcher

Pitched 47 consecutive scoreless innings

NL MVP; AL MVP that year was also a pitcher, Denny McLain—the only year the MVP Awards went to two pitchers

Recorded 17 strikeouts during Game 1 of the 1968 World Series

1970: Bob Gibson RHP (35 years old): 23–7, ERA 3.12, 274 Strikeouts

Pitched all 14 innings vs. Padres on July 20

Hit .303 in 109 at-bats

Won 23 games (his last 20-game season), win % of .767

Completed 23 of 34 games, 3 shutouts

Won Gold Glove

2005: Chris Carpenter RHP (30 years old): 21–5, ERA 2.83, 213 Strikeouts

First pitcher since 1920 to go undefeated in 16 consecutive starts, complete seven innings or more, and allow three or fewer runs in each game.

A 13-game winning streak with a 1.36 ERA over 16 starts.

22 consecutive quality starts.

Won first 12 road starts of the season, and his .923 winning percentage on the road is the highest in franchise history.

Finished with a 2.83 ERA, 213 strikeouts, seven complete games, four shutouts and a 21–5 record.

FUN FACT: Roger Clemens has the most Cy Young awards with 7; Randy Johnson is second with 5, and Steve Carlton and Greg Maddux are tied for third with 3.

COMPLETE GAMES (CG):
PITCHERS (Since 1920)

CG: WHEN A PITCHER STARTS/FINISHES THE OFFICIAL GAME.

CG (Complete Games): Single-Season Leaders

Rank	Player	Complete Games	Year
1	Dizzy Dean RHP	29	1935
2	Bob Gibson RHP	28	1968
	Bob Gibson RHP	28	1969
	Dizzy Dean RHP	28	1936
3	Dizzy Dean RHP	26	1933
4	Jesse Haines RHP	25	1927

CG (Complete Games): Career Leaders

Rank	Player	Complete Games
1	Bob Gibson RHP	255
2	Jesse Haines RHP	208
3	Dizzy Dean RHP	141
4	Bill Sherdel LHP	128
5	Harry Brecheen LHP	122

FUN FACT: The career leader in complete games is Cy Young with 749. For single-season notable performances, Bob Feller (Indians) had 36 complete games in 1946, the most since Grover Cleveland Alexander (Phillies) with 38 in 1916 and Walter Johnson (Senators) in 1910. Since 2000, the leader is James Shields (Rays) with 11 in 2011.

CLYDESDALES –
CARDINALS TRADITION: HISTORY

THE TEAM OF BUDWEISER CLYDESDALES CIRCLING THE BALLPARK
(WITH THE DALMATIAN DOG ON THE WAGON) IS A FAVORITE TRADITION IN ST. LOUIS.

BREED:

The breed was developed in the 19th century as a draft horse, used for agriculture and hauling coal, and takes its name from Clydesdale (the old name for Lanarkshire) in Scotland.

INTRODUCTION:

They were first introduced by August A. Busch Sr. and Anheuser-Busch on April 7, 1933 in celebration of the repeal of Prohibition.

NUMBERS:

Anheuser-Busch owns about 250 Clydesdales, one of the largest herds in the world; many are housed at the stables at Grant's Farm, near St. Louis.

HITCHES:

Budweiser maintains 6 hitches; five traveling and one stationary. Eight Clydesdales are hitched together to pull the wagon, two travel as back-ups.

QUALIFICATIONS:

Budweiser Clydesdale must be at least four years old (gelding), 72 inches at the shoulder, weigh between 1,800 and 2,300 pounds, and have a bay color, four white stocking feet, blaze of white on the face, and a black mane and tail.

DALMATIANS:

Dalmatians have traveled with the Clydesdale hitch since the 1950s, and were used originally to guard and protect beer deliveries.

HARNESS:

Each set of harnesses weighs 130 pounds.

WAGON:

The wagons are Studebaker wagons (circa 1900) which were converted to deliver beer.

FUN FACT: The Clydesdales have appeared in two Presidential inaugurations: for Missouri native Harry Truman's inaugural parade in 1949, and again for Bill Clinton's in 1993.

CATCHER STATS:

Catcher Stats: Offense — Single-Season Leaders

Batting Average (BA):

#1	Ted Simmons	.332	1975
#2	Yadier Molina	.319	2013
#3	Ted Simmons	.318	1977

FUN FACT: The #1 catcher in MLB for BA is Smoky Burgess (Phillies) with .368 in 1954.

On-Base Percentage (OBP):

#1	Ted Simmons	.408	1977
#2	Joe Torre	.398	1970
#3	Ted Simmons	.396	1975

FUN FACT: The #1 catcher in MLB for OBP is Mickey Cochrane (Athletics) with .459 in 1933. Note: Yankee slugger Mickey Mantle was named for Mickey Cochrane (his father's favorite player).

Runs Batted In (RBI):

#1	Ted Simmons	103	1974
#2	Joe Torre	100	1970
#3	Ted Simmons	100	1975

FUN FACT: The #1 catcher in MLB for RBI is Johnny Bench (Reds) with 148 in 1970.

Home Runs (HR):

#1	**Ted Simmons**	**26**	**1979**
#2	Yadier Molina	22	2012
#3	Ted Simmons	22	1978

FUN FACT: The #1 catcher in MLB for HR is Johnny Bench with 45 in 1970.

Wins Above Replacement (WAR):

#1	**Yadier Molina**	**6.1**	**2012**
#2	Joe Torre	6.0	1970
#3	Tim McCarver	5.9	1967

FUN FACT: The #1 catcher in MLB for WAR is Johnny Bench with 9.2 in 1972.

Catcher Stats: Defense –
Single-Season Leaders

Fielding Percentage (FP):

#1	**Mike Matheny**	**1.000**	**2003**
			(#1 that year in MLB)
#2	Mike Matheny	.999	2004
#3	Tom Pagnozzi	.999	1992

FUN FACT: In five years as catcher with the Cardinals (2000–04), Mike Matheny never had a FP lower than .994.

Putouts (PO):

#1	**Yadier Molina**	**1064**	**2015**
			(#1 that year in MLB)
#2	Yadier Molina	976	2013
#3	Yadier Molina	962	2012

FUN FACT: The #1 catcher in PO is Jiggs Donahue (White Sox) with 1846 in 1907.

Caught Stealing (CS):

#1	**Tim Pagnozzi**	**70**	**1991**
			(#1 that year in MLB)
#2	Ted Simmons	65	1978
#3	Ted Simmons	54	1977

FUN FACT: Pagnozzi is tied for #3 on the all-time MLB list; the #1 catcher in CS is Jody Davis (Cubs) with 89 in 1986.

CARDINALS COACHES

Longest-Serving CARDINALS Coaches

1. **Red Schoendienst:** 38 total seasons, with the longest streak being 23 consecutive seasons. Longest tenured coach in Cardinals' franchise history

2. **Buzzy Wares:** 23 consecutive seasons (1930–52), working under 8 different managers.

3. **Jose Oquendo,** hired in 1999 and entering his 17th season in 2016 as the Cardinals third base coach, the longest tenured current coach on the Cardinals big league staff.

4. **Dave Duncan** (pitching coach, 1996–2011) and **Dave McKay** (1st base coach, 1996–2011: 16 consecutive seasons

FUN FACT: In the early 1900s, base coaching was conducted by managers and other players. This began to change and four coaches (2 base coaches, 1 pitching, 1 hitting) became standard for many years. In 1981, MLB placed a limit of six on coaches in uniform, and then expanded to seven in 2013 with most teams adding a second hitting coach. There are more MLB managers who rose from being a third base coach, than from first base. As of 2015, six managers were former third base coaches; only John Gibbons of the Blue Jays went from first base coach to manager.

DOUBLES (2B)

Doubles (2B): Career Leaders

Rank	Career Doubles	Player
1	725	Stan Musial 1B/OF (#3 in MLB)
2	455	Albert Pujols 1B
3	434	Lou Brock LF
4	377	Joe Medwick LF
5	367	Rogers Hornsby 2B
6	366	Enos Slaughter RF
7	352	Red Schoendienst 2B
8	344	Jim Bottomley 1B
9	339	Ray Lankford CF
10	338	Ozzie Smith SS

FUN FACT: Tris Speaker (CF, Red Sox/Indians 1907–28) holds the career record for doubles with 792, Pete Rose (IF/OF Reds 1963–86) is second, and then Musial is third.

Doubles (2B): Single-Season Leaders

#1	64	Joe Medwick OF (tied for #2 in MLB)	1936
#2	56	Joe Medwick OF	1937
#3	55	Matt Carpenter 3B	2013
#4	53	Stan Musial OF	1953
#5	52	Enos Slaughter OF	1939
#6	51	Stan Musial OF	1944
#7	51	Albert Pujols 1B	2004
#8	51	Albert Pujols 1B	2003
#9	50	Stan Musial OF	1946
#10	49	Scott Rolen 3B	2003

FUN FACT: Earl Webb (RF, Red Sox) holds the record for doubles in a single season with 67 in 1931. George Burns (1B, Indians–1926) and Medwick are tied for second with 64.

DRAFT PICKS – CARDINALS

Draft Picks: Numbers Drafted by Position

BEGINNING WITH THE MLB RULE 4 DRAFT IN 1965, THE CARDS HAVE SELECTED 74 PLAYERS IN THE FIRST ROUND (THROUGH 2016):

- 30 right-handed pitchers
- 8 left-handed pitchers
- 8 outfielders
- 23 infielders
- 5 catchers

Draft Picks: History

World Series: Three first-round draft picks won World Series rings
with the Cardinals:

Braden Looper (RHP)	drafted 1996 (2006 World Series)
Chris Duncan (1B)	drafted 1999 (2006 World Series)
Lance Lynn (RHP)	drafted 2008 (2011 World Series)

FIRST Player Drafted: Joe DiFabio (RHP) drafted #20 in 1965.
DiFabio reached AA in 6 years in the Cardinals system, spent one year
with the Reds and then retired without playing in the major leagues.

FIRST Pick in the FIRST Round: The Cardinals have NEVER
had the first overall pick in the draft (team with the worst record in
baseball the previous season qualifies for the first overall pick).

Drafted in FIRST FIVE/
first-round CARDS Draft Picks:

Braden Looper RHP	3rd in 1996
Dmitri Young IF	4th in 1991
J.D. Drew OF	5th in 1998

CY YOUNG: No Cardinals first rounder has yet won the Cy Young Award.

ROY: Todd Worrell (RHP drafted 1982) is the only Cardinals first-round pick to win the Rookie Of The Year Award (1986).

Draft Picks: Other notable
Cardinal first-round picks:

Ted Simmons C	10th in 1967
Garry Templeton SS	13th in 1974
Chris Carpenter RHP	14th in 1987
Shelby Miller RHP	19th in 2009
Kolten Wong 2B	22nd in 2011
Stephen Piscotty OF	36th in 2012

FUN FACT: No first rounder drafted by the CARDS has come from Missouri; the state with the most overall draftees is California with 16.

DECADES – CARDINALS
Record by the Decade

- Decade with best winning %: *1940s*

- Decade with most 1st place titles: *2000s* (7)

- Decade with most World Series Championships: *1940s* (3)

Decade	Won-Lost (%)	1st Place Years	World Series Championships
1890s	400–707 (.361)	0	0
1900s	580–888 (.395)	0	0
1910s	652–680 (.440)	0	0
1920s	822–712 (.536)	1926, 1928	1926
1930s	869–665 (.566)	1930, 1931, 1934	1931, 1934
1940s	960–580 (.623)	1942, 1943, 1944, 1946	1942, 1944, 1946
1950s	776–763 (.504)	0	0
1960s	884–718 (.552)	1964, 1967, 1968	1964, 1967
1970s	800–813 (.496)	0	0
1980s	825–734 (.529)	1982, 1985, 1987	1982
1990s	758–794 (.488)	1996	0
2000s	913–706 (.564)	2000, 2001, 2002, 2004, 2005, 2006, 2009	2006
2010-16	637–497 (.562)	2013, 2014, 2015	2011

FUN FACT: Since 1892, the Cardinals finished first 26 times, second 19 times, and third 21 times. Their best April start was in 1968 with a 13–5 record (.722); that was the Year of the Pitcher when the Cardinals lost the World Series to the Tigers. The worst April occurred in 1973 with a 3–15 record (.167); nonetheless they ended up in 2nd place (81–81 record).

ERA (EARNED RUN AVERAGE) – PITCHERS

ERA: Starting Pitchers – Single-Season Leaders

Rank	ERA	Pitcher	Year
1	1.12	Bob Gibson RHP	1968 #1 in MLB/ modern era
2	1.72	Bill Doak RHP	1914
3	1.78	Mort Cooper RHP	1942
4	1.93	John Tudor LHP	1985
5	1.94	Max Lanier LHP	1943
6	2.02	Kid Nichols RHP	1904
7	2.03	Bugs Raymond RHP	1908
8	2.04	Ed Karger LHP	1907
9	2.09	Mike O'Neill LHP	1904
10	2.10	Howie Pollet LHP	1946
		Slim Sallee LHP	1914

FUN FACT: Since 1900, the #1 pitcher in ERA is Dutch Leonard (Boston) with 0.96 in 1914; #2 is Mordecai "Three Fingers" Brown (Cubs) with 1.04 in 1906.

ERA: Relief Pitchers — Single-Season Leaders (minimum 80 IP)

#1	1.54	Bruce Sutter RHP	1984	(122.2 IP)
#2	1.66	Al Hrabosky LHP	1975	(97.1 IP)
#3	1.84	Mike Perez RHP	1992	(93.0 IP)
#4	2.08	Todd Worrell RHP	1986	(103.2 IP)
#5	2.09	Lindy McDaniel RHP	1960	(116.1 IP)

FUN FACT: Since 1920, the #1 relief pitcher for ERA is Tim Burke (Expos) with a 1.19 ERA (91 IP) in 1987; #2 is Eric Gagne (Dodgers) with 1.20 in 2003 (82.1 IP).

ERA: Closers – Single-Season Leaders (IP/Saves)

#1	1.54	Joe Hoerner LHP	1968 (49.0 IP/17 saves)
	1.54	Bruce Sutter RHP	1984 (122.2 IP/45 saves)
#2	1.66	Al Hrabosky LHP	1975 (97.1 IP/22 saves)
#3	1.84	Jeff Lahti RHP	1985 (68.1 IP/19 saves)
#4	1.92	Seung-hwan Oh RHP	2016 (79.2 IP/19 saves)
	1.92	Ryan Franklin RHP	2009 (61.0 IP/38 saves)
#5	2.08	Todd Worrell RHP	1986 (103.2/36 saves)
#6	2.09	Lindy McDaniel RHP	1960 (116.1 IP/27 saves)
#7	2.10	Trevor Rosenthal RHP	2015 (68.2 IP/48 saves)
	2.10	Lee Smith RHP	1990 (68.2 IP/27 saves)
#8	2.14	Jason Isringhausen RHP	2005 (59.0 IP/39 saves)
#9	2.18	Bobby Shantz LHP	1962 (57.2 IP/4 saves)
#10	2.19	Mark Littell RHP	1979 (82.1 IP/13 saves)

FUN FACT: New York Giants Manager John McGraw was one of the first managers to use a relief pitcher in 1905, though it took some years to really expand. Five pitchers who were primarily relievers have been elected to the Hall of Fame (HOF): Hoyt Wilhelm (1985), Rollie Fingers (1992), Dennis Eckersley (1992), Bruce Sutter (2006), and Goose Gossage (2008). Eckersley is considered the first "one–inning save closer" to have been elected.

ERA-MINUS (ERA-) – SINCE 1920

ERA-MINUS IS A STAT THAT FACTORS IN THE BALLPARK AND THE LEAGUE AVERAGE ERA.

Numbers: Excellent–70, Great–80, Above Average–90, Average–100. Below Average–110, Poor–115, Awful–125. Check out fangraphs. com for more information.

ERA-minus: Career Leaders – Starting Pitchers

Rank	Pitcher	ERA-
1	Mort Cooper RHP	74
1	Max Lanier LHP	74
2	Harry Brecheen LHP	75
2	Dizzy Dean RHP	75
3	Chris Carpenter RHP	76
4	Howie Pollet LHP	78
4	Bob Gibson RHP	78
5	Adam Wainwright RHP	80

ERA-minus: Single-Season Leaders – Starting Pitchers

#1	Bob Gibson RHP	38	1968 (#1 in MLB)
#2	Mort Cooper RHP	53	1942
#3	John Tudor LHP	55	1985
	Harry Brecheen LHP	55	1948
#4	Steve Carlton LHP	60	1969
#5	Bob Gibson RHP	61	1969
	Howie Pollet LHP	61	1946

FUN FACT: Pedro Martinez (Red Sox) is the #1 career leader in ERA-minus with 67; Clayton Kershaw (Dodgers), who is still active, currently has 63. The single-season #1, per above, is Bob Gibson with 38 in 1968; Dwight Gooden (Mets) is #2 with 44 in 1985. Of active pitchers, Zach Greinke (Dodgers in 2015) and Jake Arrieta (Cubs in 2015) are currently at #3 in MLB with 45, tied with Roger Clemens (Blue Jays in 1998), and Pedro Martinez (Expos in 1997).

EAGLE SIGN AT
BUSCH STADIUM *(Retired as of 1996)*

The **Anheuser-Busch neon eagle** in left center field was taken down in advance of the 1996 season, replaced by a bank advertisement, reportedly because it was difficult to maintain. This left St. Louis with only the one neon eagle overlooking Highway 40 (such a beautiful sign, erected in 1962). There is only one other left at Anheuser-Busch's brewery in Newark, New Jersey.

The sign originated with the renovation of Busch Stadium I in 1953–54. The eagle would flap its wings anytime a home run was hit.

The eagles (five total) were made beginning in 1953 by Artkraft Strauss, who also made the original Busch Stadium scoreboard in 1966. Artkraft hired a Disney animator named Byron Rabbit to create the sign. He studied his own rented eagle to perfect the sign's flight movement.

Since 2006, there is a new Budweiser scoreboard sign at Busch Stadium III, which is uniquely placed with the Arch in the background.

FUN FACT: Other ballparks with famous architecture include Fenway's Green Monster, Wrigley Field's Red Sign, and the newer Pepsi Bottle at the Giant's AT&T Park.

ERRORS

FUN FACT: The #1 in single-season errors since 1934 is Al Brancato SS (Athletics) with 61 in 1941; Arky Vaughan SS (Pittsburg) is #2 with 52. The Cardinals had their fewest team errors in 2003 with 77.

Errors: Most Career

#1	Marty Marion SS	247
#2	Ken Boyer 3B	225
#3	Julian Javier 2B	219
#4	Rogers Hornsby 2B	207
#5	Ozzie Smith SS	196

FUN FACT: The #1 in career errors (since 1920) is Luke Appling SS (White Sox 1930–50) with 643. The fewest career errors since 1920: #1 is Vernon Wells (11,812 innings with the Blue Jays, etc., 1999–2013) with 20. Of note, the legendary Mickey Mantle had only 40 errors in his career.

Errors: Most Career by Position

C	Ted Simmons	104
1B	Jim Bottomley	174
2B	Julian Javier	219
SS	Marty Marion	247
3B	Ken Boyer	225
LF	Lou Brock	167
CF	Willie McGee	72
RF	Joe Cunningham	24
P	Ted Breitenstein	44

FUN FACT: The pitcher with the most career errors is Cy Young with 131; Joe McGinnity is second with 100. On the other side, the catcher who has the most errors is Bob Boone with 178; Jason Kendall is second with 144.

Errors: TEAM Best/Worst by Season:

Best/Fewest:	#1	75	2013
	#2	77	2003
	#3	80	1994
Worst/Most:	#1	204	1920
	#2	190	1923
	#3	186	1922

FUN FACT: Since 2006, the Cardinals' worst season for errors was 2007 with 121; in 2016, the team had 106. The #1 team with the most errors in one season is the Phillies with 235 in 1921; the Orioles hold the record for fewest errors with 54 in 2013.

is for...

FIRSTS – CARDINALS:

- **First inducted into the Hall of Fame (HOF):**
  Rogers Hornsby 2B

- **First MVP or equivalent ("National League Award"):**
  Rogers Hornsby 2B (1925)

- **First Triple Crown Award (batting):** Rogers Hornsby
  2B (1922)

- **First World Series Championship:** 1926

- **First Cy Young Award:** Bob Gibson (1968)

- **First Rookie of the Year Award:** Wally Moon OF (1954)

- **First Gold Glove Award:** Ken Boyer 3B (1958)

- **First Platinum Glove Award:** Yadier Molina C (2011)

- **First Silver Slugger Awards:** —1980 (4 CARDS)—Bob
  Forsch P, Ted Simmons C, Keith Hernandez 1B, and George
  Hendrick OF

- **First Roberto Clemente Award:** Ozzie Smith SS (1995)

- **First Manager of the Year:** Whitey Herzog (1985)

- **First World Series MVP:** Bob Gibson P (1967)

- **First NLCS (National League Conference Series) MVP:** Darrell Porter C (1982)

- **First ALL-STAR Game in St. Louis:** July 9, 1940 at Sportsman's Park

- **First National League (NL) Pitcher to 3,000 strikeouts:** Bob Gibson (1974)

FRANCHISE LEADERS: BATTING

Franchise Leaders/Batting – Career:

Category	Statistic	Player
BA (Batting Average)	.358	Rogers Hornsby 2B (1915–26, 1933)
H (Hits)	3,630	Stan Musial OF/1B (1,815 home/1,815 road)
2B/Doubles	725	Stan Musial OF/1B
3B/Triples	177	Stan Musial OF/1B
HR (Home Runs)	475	Stan Musial OF/1B
RBI (Runs Batted In)	1,951	Stan Musial OF/1B
BB (Walks)	1,599	Stan Musial OF/1B
SB (Stolen Bases)	888	Lou Brock LF
Games	3,026	Stan Musial OF/1B

Franchise Leaders/Batting – Single Season:

BA (Batting Average):	.424	Rogers Hornsby 2B (1924)
HR (Home Runs):	70	Mark McGwire 1B (1998)
Hits:	250	Rogers Hornsby 2B (1922)
XBH (Extra Base Hits):	103	Stan Musial OF (1948)
RBI (Runs Batted In):	154	Joe Medwick LF (1937)
OBP (On Base %):	.507	Rogers Hornsby 2B (1924)
Slugging %:	.756	Rogers Hornsby 2B (1925)
OPS (OBP + Slugging):	1.245	Rogers Hornsby 2B (1925)
BB (Walks):	162	Mark McGwire 1B (1998)
SB (Stolen Bases):	118	Lou Brock LF (1974)
1B (Singles):	181	Jesse Burkett OF (1901)
2B (Doubles):	64	Joe Medwick LF (1936)
3B (Triples):	25	Tom Long SS (1915)
Runs Scored:	142	Jesse Burkett OF (1901)
IBB (Intentional Walks):	44	Albert Pujols 1B (2009)
HBP (Hit by Pitch):	31	Steve Evans OF (1910)
KO (Strikeouts):	167	Jim Edmonds CF (2000)
SAC (Sacrifice Bunts):	37	Taylor Douthit CF (1926)
SF (Sacrifice Flies):	14	George Hendrick OF (1982)
TB (Total Bases):	450	Rogers Hornsby 2B (1922)
NP (# of Pitches):	3101	Matt Carpenter 3B (2014)
PA (Plate Appearances):	752	Taylor Douthit CF (1928)
CS (Caught Stealing):	33	Lou Brock OF (1974)

FRANCHISE LEADERS: PITCHING

Franchise Leaders/Pitching – Career (minimum 1,500 innings pitched)		
W (Wins):	250	Bob Gibson
ERA (Earned Run Average):	2.67	Slim Sallee
KO (Strikeouts):	3,099	Bob Gibson
SHO (Shutouts):	56	Bob Gibson
IP (Innings Pitched):	3,866	Bob Gibson

Franchise Leaders/Starting Pitchers – Single Season

Category	Statistic	Player
W (Wins)	30	Dizzy Dean (1934)
ERA (Earned Run Average)	1.12	Bob Gibson (1968)
KO (Strikeouts)	274	Bob Gibson (1970)
SHO (Shutouts)	13	Bob Gibson (1968)
IP (Innings Pitched)	447.1	Ted Breitenstein (1894)
K% (Strikeout %)	23.4	Adam Wainwright (2010)
CG (Complete Games)	46	Ted Breitenstein (1894 & 1895)

Franchise Leaders/Relief Pitchers – Single Season

SV (Saves):	48	Trevor Rosenthal (2015)
ERA (Earned Run Average):	1.54	Bruce Sutter (1984)
	1.54	Joe Hoerner (1966)
K-BB% (Strikeout-Walk%):	28.3	Trevor Rosenthal (2013)
K% (Strikeout%):	34.7	Trevor Rosenthal (2013)

FIELDING: CARDINALS LEADERS
BY POSITION – SINGLE SEASON

POS.	Player	Year	G	TC	E	%
C	Mike Matheny	2003	138	823	0	1.000
1B	Keith Hernandez	1981	98	1,143	3	.997
1B	Tino Martinez	2003	126	1,114	3	.997
2B	Jose Oquendo	1990	150	681	3	.996
SS	Ozzie Smith	1991	150	639	8	.987
3B	Troy Glaus	2008	146	385	7	.982
OF	Curt Flood	1966	159	396	0	1.000
OF	Orlando Palmeiro	2003	112	171	0	1.000
OF	Jon Jay	2012	116	292	0	1.000
OF	Ray Lankford	1996	144	366	1	.997
OF	Tony Scott	1980	134	330	1	.997

FUN FACT: In addition to 2003 above, Mike Matheny had a .999 fielding percentage in 2004.

CURT FLOOD &
THE RESERVE CLAUSE

Curt Flood was CF for the Cardinals 1958–69. He had a career batting average of .293, with 1,861 hits and 636 RBI; in 1967, his batting average was .335.

He was a 3-time Cardinals All-Star (1964, 66, 68), Gold Glove Award winner 7 times, and World Series champion in 1964 and 1967.

Reserve Clause: On October 7, 1969, Flood was traded with Tim McCarver, Byron Browne, and Joe Hoerner to the Phillies. Flood was unhappy with the trade and decided to pursue legal options, arguing

that he was not "property to be bought and sold" without his permission, and that he should be allowed to consider options with any of the Major League clubs via free agency. Flood's case challenging the "reserve clause" against Baseball Commissioner Bowie Kuhn (Flood v. Kuhn), went before the U.S. Supreme Court in 1972, and the Court ruled in favor of Major League Baseball and Kuhn.

Impact on Flood: Flood was blackballed from baseball, sitting out the entire 1970 season, and he received hate mail and death threats from upset fans. In 1971, he signed with the Senators under manager Ted Williams, but after 13 games, he decided to retire.

Curt Flood Act of 1998: 26 years later, the ruling was finally changed to stop owners from controlling the players' contracts and careers.

Flood returned to baseball in 1978 as a member of the Athletics broadcasting team, and in 1988 was named commissioner of the Senior Professional Baseball Association (SPBA) which did not last very long. He passed away in 1995 at age 59 but left behind a huge legacy benefiting all professional baseball players.

is for...

GRAND SLAMS

First Grand Slam: Roger Connor 1B (then with the Troy Trojans of the NL) hit the first in 1881. He was the original home run champion before Babe Ruth. Later, with the New York Gothams, Connor reportedly helped contribute to their name change to the "Giants" thanks to his size. The term "grand slam" comes from contract bridge.

Grand Slams: Cardinals Leaders – Single Season

#1	Albert Pujols 1B	5	2009
#2	Jim Bottomley 2B	3	1925
	Keith Hernandez 1B	3	1977
	Fernando Tatis 3B	3	1999

FUN FACT: Travis Hafner (Indians–2006) and Don Mattingly (Yankees–1987) are tied for most single-season grand slams with 6. Pujols is #1 in the NL, tied with Ernie Banks (Cubs–1955), with 5.

Grand Slams:
CARDINALS Leaders – Career

#1	Albert Pujols 1B	12	2001–11
#2	Stan Musial 1B/OF	9	1941–63
#3	Rogers Hornsby 2B	7	1915–26, 1933
	Ken Boyer 3B	7	1955–65
	Ted Simmons C	7	1968–80

FUN FACT: Alex Rodriguez (Yankees) is #1 in career grand slams with 25

Grand Slams (GS): Notable Cardinals

MLB Most GS in 1 Single Inning: 2 – Fernando Tatis

Tatis (3B) hit 2 in the 3rd inning on April 23, 1999 vs. Chan Ho Park (Dodgers). Tatis also set the MLB record for RBI in one inning with 8 RBI during that inning.

MLB Most GS by a Pitcher (Career): 2 – Bob Gibson

Cardinals RHP *Bob Gibson* is tied with Madison Bumgarner (LHP Giants) and 6 others for the MLB record.

NL Team Most in One Season: 12 – Cardinals in 2000 (tied with Braves, 12 in 1997)

Only Cardinal with a GS in a World Series: 1 – Ken Boyer 3B (1964).

Boyer hit a grand slam in Game 4 off Yankee pitcher Al Downing, giving the Cards a 4–3 victory. There have been 18 GS in the World Series.

FUN FACT: Two players have hit a grand slam on the 1st pitch of their 1st MLB at bat: Kevin Kouzmanoff 3B (Indians – September 2, 1996) and Daniel Nava LF (Red Sox – June 12, 2010)

Grand Slams:
by CARDINALS Pitchers (SINCE 1900)

Year	Pitcher	Date/Game
1902	Mike O'Neill	June 3, at Boston
1938	Curt Davis	April 26, at Cincinnati
1965	Bob Gibson	September 29, at San Francisco
1973	Bob Gibson	July 26, vs. New York
1973	Rick Wise	August 21, at Atlanta
1984	Rick Andujar	May 15, vs. Atlanta
1986	Bob Forsch	August 10, vs. Pittsburgh
1996	Donovan Osborne	September 7, vs. San Diego
1998	Kent Mercker	September 2, at Florida
2009	Chris Carpenter	October 1, at Cincinnati
2010	Brad Penny	May 21, vs. Los Angeles/AL
2011	Jake Westbrook	August 31, at Milwaukee

FUN FACT: Giants pitcher Madison Bumgarner hit his two career grand slams in one season (2014).

GOLD GLOVE &
PLATINUM GLOVE AWARDS

Gold/Platinum Gloves: notable Cardinals

Ozzie Smith: 13 Gold

#1 in MLB for most Gold Gloves at SS

Bob Gibson: 9 Gold

#3 in MLB for Gold Gloves as a Pitcher

Yadier Molina: 4 Platinum

#1 in MLB for most Platinum Gold Gloves with 4 (only catcher to win) in 2011, 2012, 2014, and 2015. The Platinum Gold Glove started in 2011.

Wainwright/Molina
Battery-Mate Winners: 2 (2009 & 2013)

Yadier Molina C and Adam Wainwright P won Gold Gloves in 2009 and 2013, an MLB record. Ivan Rodriguez C and Kenny Rogers P, also won twice together but on two different teams: 2000 for the Rangers, and 2006 for the Tigers.

Gold Gloves: CARDINAL Winners

11	Ozzie Smith SS (#1 at SS in MLB)
9	Bob Gibson P
8	Yadier Molina C
7	Curt Flood OF
6	Jim Edmonds OF
6	Keith Hernandez 1B
6	Bill White 1B
5	Ken Boyer 3B
4	Scott Rolen 3B
3	Willie McGee OF
3	Bobby Shantz P
3	Tom Pagnozzi C
3	Mike Matheny C
2	Adam Wainwright P
2	Albert Pujols 1B
2	Terry Pendleton 3B
2	Fernando Vina 2B
2	Edgar Renteria SS
1	Joaquin Andujar P
1	Ken Reitz 3B
1	Dal Maxvill SS
1	Jayson Heyward OF

FUN FACT: Created in 1957 by glove manufacturer Rawlings, Gold Gloves were initially awarded to the top MLB 9 positions (#1 overall) and then expanded to 9 positions in each league (18 total – National and American Leagues). Pitcher Greg Maddux has won the most with 18, including 13 consecutive awards from 1990 to 2002.

GAME SCORE (GS): STARTING PITCHERS

Game Score: What is it? The "game score" evaluates the starting pitcher's performance and is usually included in the box score.

- *Calculation:* Start with 50 points (pts)

- *+Add:* 1 point for each out recorded, 2 points each inning completed after the 4th , and 1 point for each strikeout.

- *-Subtract:* 2 points for each hit allowed, 4 points for each earned run allowed, 2 points for each unearned run allowed, and 1 point for each walk.

- *Total:* Game Score

FUN FACT: The maximum score is 114: 50 + 27 (outs) + 10 (10 points for innings after 4th) + 27 (strikeouts).

Game Score: 90+ Game Leaders (100+ Games Score Games)

Rank	Pitcher	90+ Games	100+ Games
1	Nolan Ryan	31	4
2	Randy Johnson	20	1
3	Sandy Koufax	18	1
4	Tom Seaver	16	1
5	Bob Gibson	14	1

Game Score: Bob Gibson 100-Point Game

July 25, 1969 at Busch Stadium:

Cards 2, Giants 1 (complete 13-inning game)

Gibson Performance:

6 hits
1 earned run
2 walks
11 strikeouts
2.34 ERA

Gibson was facing Gaylord Perry, who had pitched a no-hitter against Gibson and the Cards the year before on September 17, 1968 (Gibson struck out 10 but lost the game on a Ron Hunt home run). Gibson got even in 1969 with the game 1–1 after the first and continuing through 12 innings, with both Gibson and Perry still on the mound. Perry was relieved by Frank Linzy in the 13th; his first batter was Gibson who singled, and came around to score the winning run.

FUN FACT: Thirteen times, pitchers have achieved 100 or higher in a 9-inning game. Kerry Wood (Cubs) holds the record with 105 in his 20K game in 1998. Max Scherzer (Nationals) is second (and the most recent) with 104 in a no-hitter against the Mets in October 2015; that was also the highest score achieved in a no-hitter.

"GASHOUSE GANG" — Early 1930s
CARDS Team (*1934 World Series Champions*)

Gashouse Gang: Nickname Origin

Gashouse: "The name described the enjoyment with which they seemed to play the game, along with the aggressive attitude they took that always seemed to give them dirty uniforms, making them resemble the grease-stained clothing worn by car mechanics." (baseballreference.com)

Gashouse Gang:
Prominent members of the 1934 team

5 players hit .300 or above during the regular 1934 season:

Ripper Collins 1B	*.330*
Frankie Frisch 2B	.305
Joe Medwick OF	.319
Spud Davis C	.300
Ernie Orsatti OF	.300

Gashouse Gang:
Stat Leaders in 1934 (MLB/NL)

Ripper Collins (1B):

.615 slugging % (#1 NL), 1.008 OPS (#1 NL), 35 home runs (#1 NL), 87 extra base hits (#1 NL), 369 total bases (#1 NL), and 144 runs created (#1 NL). Collins also had 128 RBI (#2 NL).

Joe Medwick OF:

18 triples (#1 MLB)

Pepper Martin 3B:

23 stolen bases (#1 NL)

Dizzy Dean P:

30 wins (#1 MLB), 195 strikeouts (#1 MLB), 7 shutouts (#1 MLB), 8.5 WAR for pitchers (#1 MLB), 5.786 strikeouts per 9 innings (#1 MLB), .811 win–loss % (#1 NL)

Gashouse GANG

Regular season: 95–58 (.621).

Dizzy Dean (P) won the MVP award. Branch Rickey was the General Manager, and Frankie Frisch the Manager. Dizzy Dean won 30 games (the last NL pitcher to win 30 games); Daffy Dean 19.

World Series:

Cards 4, Tigers 3. The third Cards championship in nine years. This was the last World Series in which both teams were led by player-managers (Frisch for the Cards, and Mickey Cochrane for the Tigers).

World Series Pitching:

During the World Series, Dizzy and Daffy Dean each had two of the four wins to defeat the Tigers with 28 strikeouts and a 1.43 ERA. The Cards used only 8 pitchers during the 7-game series.

World Series Hitting:

Joe Medwick (OF) batted .379, Ripper Collins (1B) .367, and Pepper Martin (3B) .355. Medwick also had a series-high 5 RBI and a home run.

World Series HOFers:

Cards – Dizzy Dean, Leo Durocher, Frankie Frisch, Jesse Haines, Joe Medwick, and Dazzy Vance. Tigers – Mickey Cochrane, Charlie Gehringer, Goose Goslin, Hank Greenberg. Umpire: Bill Klem.

Don Gutteridge (2B/3B/SS):

the last surviving member of the "Gashouse" 30s team died in 2008; his MLB debut with the Cardinals was in 1936. At the time of his death at age 96, he was the oldest living former MLB coach/manager, and also the last living St. Louis Brown who played in their only World Series in 1944.

Further reading:

"The Gashouse Gang" by John Heidenry (2007).

FUN FACT: Since the Cardinals–Tigers match-up in the 1934 World Series, they have met two other times. In 1968, the "Year of the Pitcher," the Tigers' Denny McLain was the first pitcher to win 30-plus games (he had 31 wins) since Dizzy Dean in 1934. The Tigers defeated the Cards that year. The other time was in 2006 when the Cards beat the Tigers in five games.

HALL OF FAME (HOF) CARDINALS – COOPERSTOWN:

Stan Musial and Bob Gibson are two of the 49 players elected who played for only one team in their MLB career.

A number of other former Cardinals have been elected, either having selected another team as their primary (for example, Joe Torre), or being associated with multiple teams (for example, Branch Rickey).

HOF: 17 CARDINALS (by induction year)

- 17 players have been inducted with the Cardinals being their primary team:

- 3 Managers (the most recent inductees), 6 infielders, 5 outfielders, 3 pitchers:

Rogers Hornsby 2B (1942)	Frankie Frisch 2B (1947)
Dizzy Dean P (1953)	Chick Hafey OF (1971)

Jim Bottomley 1B (1974)	Bob Gibson P (1981)
Lou Brock LF (1985)	Joe Medwick LF (1968)
Stan Musial OF/1B (1969)	Jesse Haines P (1970)
Johnny Mize 1B (1981)	Enos Slaughter RF (1985)
Red Schoendienst 2B (1989)	Ozzie Smith SS (2002)
Billy Southworth Mgr (2008)	Whitey Herzog Mgr (2010)
Tony La Russa Mgr (2014)	

FUN FACT: Rogers Hornsby 2B was the only HOF electee in 1942 (with 78.1% of the vote), and the first to be inducted since 1939, as no elections were held in 1940 or 1941. The first players to be elected to the Hall of Fame in 1936: Ty Cobb (CF–Tigers), Walter Johnson (P–Senators), Christy Mathewson (P–Giants), Babe Ruth (OF–Yankees), and Honus Wagner (SS–Pirates).

HOME RUNS (HR) – CARDINALS

(see "G" for grand slams)

HR: Longest HRs at Busch Stadium III

#1	Brandon Moss	477 feet	6/30/2016	Deep RF
#2	Matt Holliday	469 feet	7/20/2012	Left CF Beyond Bleachers
#3	Matt Holliday	467 feet	9/12/2014	Big Mac land

FUN FACT: Longest HR in history? Challenging subject. Mickey Mantle started the "tape measure" HR with the 1953 shot at Griffith Stadium estimated at 565 feet, and his 1963 blast that struck the top façade of Yankee Stadium. More recent home runs are easier with MLB Statcast (2015/16): Giancarlo Stanton (Marlins) hit one 504 feet on 8/16/2016 and Kris Bryant (Cubs) went 495 feet on 9/6/2015.

HR: Single-Season Leaders – with Walks (BB)/Strikeouts(K)

#1	70	Mark McGwire 1B	(1998)	162BB/155K
#2	65	Mark McGwire 1B	(1999)	133BB/141K
#3	49	Albert Pujols 1B	(2006)	92BB/50K
#4	47	Albert Pujols 1B	(2009)	115BB/64K
#5	46	Albert Pujols 1B	(2004)	84BB/52K
#6	43	Johnny Mize 1B	(1940)	82BB/49K
#7	43	Albert Pujols 1B	(2003)	79BB/65K
#8	42	Jim Edmonds CF	(2004)	101BB/150K
#9	42	Jim Edmonds CF	(2000)	103BB/167K
#10	42	Rogers Hornsby 2B	(1922)	65BB/50K

FUN FACT: Barry Bonds (Giants) is #1 in HR with 73 in 2001, McGwire is #2 (70), and Sammy Sosa (Cubs) is #3 (66). IN 2016, the Cards had 6 players with 20 or more home runs: Matt Carpenter (21), Stephen Piscotty (22), Jedd Gyorko (30), Randal Grichuk (24), Matt Holliday (20), and Brandon Moss (28). The 2016 team was #1 in the NL for HR with 225 and #2 in Cards club history. The #1 season for team HR was 2000 with 235 home runs.

HR: Most 30+ Seasons 1925–1940:

2	Rogers Hornsby 2B (1922, 1925)
1	Johnny Mize 1B (1940)
1	Jim Bottomley 1B (1928)
1	Ripper Collins 1B (1934)

HR: Most 30+ Seasons 1940–Present:

11	Albert Pujols 1B
6	Stan Musial 1B/OF
4	Jim Edmonds CF

FUN FACT: Cardinals switch-hitter Mark Whiten RF hit 4 Home Runs in one game on September 7, 1993 against the Reds. Only 10 NL and 6 AL players have hit 4 HR in one game.

HR: In First Major League At-Bat!

1936	Eddie Morgan 1B/RF	(opening day – first pitch, pinch-hit)
1954	Wally Moon OF	(opening day)
2000	Chris Richard 1B/OF	(first pitch)
2001	Gene Stechschulte P	(first pitch, pinch-hit)
2004	Hector Luna IF	(second pitch)
2006	Adam Wainwright P	(first pitch)
2008	Mark Worrell P	(full count)

FUN FACT: HOF pitcher Hoyt Wilhelm hit a home run in his first major league at-bat, never to hit one again during his career. The HR on first at-bat has happened 119 times in MLB, the most recent being 3 in 2016: Wilson Contreras (Cubs), Tyler Austin (Yankees), and Aaron Judge (Yankees).

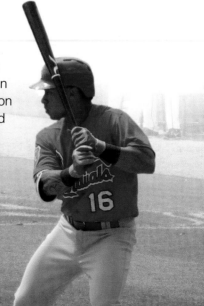

HR: Inside-the-Park
CARDINALS Leaders (Career)

Rank	Player	Inside-the-Park HR's
1	Rogers Hornsby 2B	30
2	Ed Konetchy 1B	22
3	Jesse Burkett LF	19

FUN FACT: #3 above, LF Jesse Burkett, is the Cardinals' single-season leader for inside-the-park HRs with 8 in 1901.

HR: CARDINALS
Pinch-Hit HR in First MLB At -Bat

"Pinch Hit" – from baseball writers in 1905 when legendary Giants Manager John McGraw had switch-hitter Sammy Strang fill in, "in a pinch," fourteen times.

Eddie Morgan RF	1936	7th inning – April 14, 1936
Gene Stechschulte P	2001	6th inning – April 17, 2001

FUN FACT: Frenchy Bordagaray (OF/IF)—great name!—is #4 in MLB for highest batting average by a pinch hitter with .465 (minimum 30 at-bats) in 1938; he played for the Cards in 1937 and 1938. Frenchy was a colorful character and sported a mustache at a time when players were expected to be clean shaven:

I was making $3,000 a year playing baseball so I figured I could at least have fun while I was not getting rich. But after I had (the mustache) about two months, Casey (Stengel) called me into the clubhouse and said, 'If anyone's going to be a clown on this club, it's going to be me.'" (Frenchy Bordagaray)

HR: Team Pinch-Hits Home Runs – new #1 MLB Records by Cardinals

17   Pinch-hit HRs in 2016 – #1 in MLB history
Cardinals set new MLB single-season record with
17 in 2016 (previous record 14 in 2001 by the
Diamondbacks and Giants)

3   Pinch hits in one game (April 8, 2016) – #1 in MLB
history

FUN FACT: The 17th pinch-hit home run was served up by Matt
Holliday on September 30, 2016, after being activated off the DL so fans
at Busch Stadium could bid their 7-time All-Star goodbye. Holliday was
greeted with a standing ovation and then launched one off Pirates reliever
Zach Phillips, over the right-field wall. It was the first pinch-hit home run
of Holliday's 13-year career.

HITS (H):

Hits: TOP 5 Career Leaders

Rank	Career Hits	Player
1	3,630	Stan Musial OF (#4 on all-time MLB list)
2	3,023	Lou Brock OF
3	2,110	Rogers Hornsby 2B
4	2,073	Albert Pujols 1B
5	2,064	Enos Slaughter RF

FUN FACT: Stan Musial hit exactly half of his 3,630 hits at home and
exactly half away; 1,815 each! Per above, Stan Musial and Lou Brock are
the only two Cardinals so far with 3,000 hits.

Hits: TOP 5 Single-Season Leaders

Rank	Single-Season Hits	Player	Year
1	250	Rogers Hornsby 2B	1922 (#3 over in the NL)
2	237	Joe Medwick OF	1937
3	235	Rogers Hornsby 2B	1921
4	230	Stan Musial OF	1948
4	230	Joe Torre 3B	1971
5	228	Stan Musial OF	1946

FUN FACT: The single-season MLB leader in hits is Ichiro Suzuki RF (Mariners) with 262 in 2004.

Hits: Six Hits in One Game – Since 1900 (9-inning game)

1924	Jim Bottomley 1B	(September 16 at Dodgers)
1931	Jim Bottomley 1B	(August 5 at Pirates)
1935	Terry Moore CF	(September 5 vs. Red Sox)

FUN FACT: There are only two 7-hit games in history (9 innings): Wilbert Robinson (Baltimore–1892) and Rennie Stennet (Pittsburgh–1975).

Hits: Hit for the Cycle – 16 CARDINALS

(NOTE: IN ONE GAME, HIT A SINGLE, DOUBLE, TRIPLE, AND HOME RUN – IN ANY ORDER)

Cliff Heathcote (OF)	July 13, 1918 vs. Phillies
Jim Bottomley (1B)	July 15, 1927 vs. Phillies
Chick Hafey (OF)	August 21, 1930 vs. Phillies
Pepper Martin (3B)	May 5, 1933 vs. Phillies

Joe Medwick (LF)	June 29, 1935 vs. Reds
Johnny Mize (1B)	July 13, 1940 vs. Giants
Stan Musial (1B)	July 24, 1949 vs. Dodgers
Bill White (1B)	Aug 14, 1960 vs. Pirates
Ken Boyer (3B)	Sept 14, 1961 vs. Cubs
Ken Boyer (3B)	June 16, 1964 vs. Houston
Joe Torre (3B)	June 27, 1973 vs. Pirates
Lou Brock (LF)	May 27, 1975 vs. Padres
Willie McGee (OF)	June 23, 1984 vs. Cubs
Ray Lankford (OF)	September 15, 1991 vs. Mets
John Mabry (1B)	May 18, 1996 vs. Rockies
Mark Grudzielanek (IF)	April 27, 2005 vs. Brewers

FUN FACT: Only 4 players have hit for the cycle three times in their MLB careers: John Reilly (Reds – hit the third in 1890), Bob Meusel (Yankees – third one in 1928), Babe Herman (Robins/Cubs – third one in 1933), and Adrian Beltre (Mariners/Rangers – third one in 2015). The youngest player to hit for the cycle is Mike Trout, at age 21 (Angels – 2013).

Hits: Hit for the Cycle/Natural – 2 CARDINALS

(NOTE: HIT FOR THE CYCLE/NATURAL IS IN ORDER OF SINGLE, DOUBLE, TRIPLE, AND HOME RUN.)

Ken Boyer 3B	1964
John Mabry 1B	1996

FUN FACT: There have been 14 players (from 10 teams) who have hit for a natural cycle in MLB history, the most recent being Brad Wilkerson (OF) of the Montreal Expos on June 24, 2003. Twenty teams are without a natural cycle on the books.

#1	Rogers Hornsby (2B)	33 Games (1922) – 19th in MLB (tied)
#2	Stan Musial (OF/1B)	30 Games (1950)
	Albert Pujols (1B)	30 Games (2003)

FUN FACT: Joe DiMaggio (OF Yankees) holds the MLB record with 56 games in 1941.

HOLLIDAY, MATT – CARDINAL OF 2009–2016

- Raised in Stillwater, Oklahoma, Matt's father (Tom Holliday) and brother (Josh Holliday) are college baseball coaches.

- Drafted by the Rockies in the 7th round in 1998, Holliday made his debut vs. the Cardinals on April 16, 2004.

- Switched his uniform number to 7 in January 2010 in honor of fellow Oklahoman Mickey Mantle.

- Fifth player in MLB history to put up 9 consecutive seasons of at least 20 HR, 30 doubles, 75 RBI, and 80 runs scored each season.

- Hit the longest home run of the season at Busch Stadium in each of 3 years (2012–14).Cardinals All-Star 2009–2013, 2015.

- Hit his first career pinch-hit home run on October 1, 2016, coming back off the disabled list; made one last appearance in LF in the 9th on October 2, 2016 to a standing ovation.

FUN FACT: During his time with the Cardinals, Holliday posted the following stats: .292 batting average (career .303), 616 RBI, 1,048 hits, 156 home runs, and .874 OPS (.380 OBP and .494 slugging percentage).

IRONMEN CARDINALS

Ironmen/Most Games – Single Season

#1	163	Jose Oquendo 2B (1989) (extra tie-breaker games that year)
#2	162	Ken Boyer 3B (1964)
		Curt Flood OF (1964)
		Pedro Guerrero 1B (1989)
		Terry Pendleton 3B (1989)
		Bill White 1B (1963)
#3	161	Dick Groat SS (1964)
		Keith Hernandez 1B (1977 & 79)
		Julian Javier 2B (1963)
		Albert Pujols 1B (2001 & 05)
		Ken Reitz 3B (1979)
		Ted Simmons C (1973)
		Joe Torre 3B (1970 & 71)

FUN FACT: Maury Wills (IF Dodgers) is #1 in the NL for most games played in a season with 165 in 1962; that year the Dodgers had a three-game playoff that counted in the regular season (the Giants won).

Ironmen/Most Games – Career

Rank	Career Games	Player
1	3,026	Stan Musial OF (tied #6 in MLB)
2	2,289	Lou Brock LF
3	1,990	Ozzie Smith SS
4	1,820	Enos Slaughter RF
5	1,795	Red Schoendienst 2B
6	1,738	Curt Flood OF
7	1,705	Albert Pujols 1B
8	1,667	Ken Boyer 3B
9	1,661	Willie McGee CF
10	1,580	Rogers Hornsby 2B Ray Lankford CF

FUN FACT: Pete Rose (Reds) is #1 in MLB with 3,562 career games; Musial is tied with Eddie Murray (Orioles) at #6 (3,026). Ty Cobb (Tigers) was the first to reach 3,000 games.

Jose Oquendo played for the Cardinals from 1986–95, and has coached since 1986.

- Most Games Played/#1 NL – Single Season: 163 in 1989 season (see above)

- Longest Serving: Oquendo is the longest-tenured 3rd base coach in MLB history

- Played ALL 9 positions in 1988, including pitcher and catcher (since 2000)

- #1 in MLB for fewest errors at 2B (3) in 1990

- #1 in NL – Fielding %/2B: 1989 (.994) and 1990 (.996)

- #1 in NL – Range Factor/Game as 2B: 1989 (5.42)

- #1 in NL – Range Factor/9 Innings as 2B: 1989 (5.60) and 1991 (5.87)

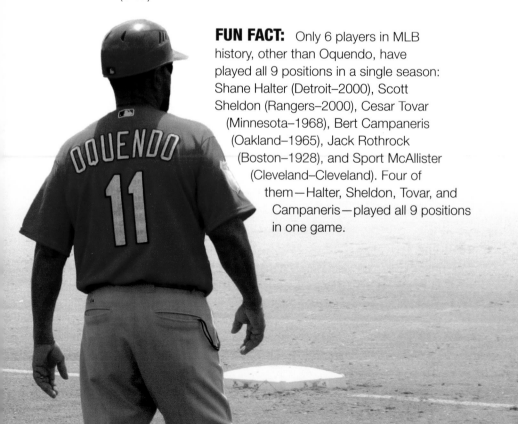

FUN FACT: Only 6 players in MLB history, other than Oquendo, have played all 9 positions in a single season: Shane Halter (Detroit–2000), Scott Sheldon (Rangers–2000), Cesar Tovar (Minnesota–1968), Bert Campaneris (Oakland–1965), Jack Rothrock (Boston–1928), and Sport McAllister (Cleveland–Cleveland). Four of them—Halter, Sheldon, Tovar, and Campaneris—played all 9 positions in one game.

IMMACULATE INNINGS:
Striking out 3 Batters on 9 Pitches/9 Strikes

Two Cardinal Pitchers:

Bob Gibson: May 12, 1969 vs. Dodgers 7th inning, 6–2 win
(Striking out: Len Gabrielson, PaulPopovich, John Miller)

Jason Isringhausen: April 13, 2002 vs. Astros 9th inning,
(Striking out: Daryle Ward, Jose Vizcaino, Julio Lugo)

Have the Cardinals ever suffered their own immaculate inning? Yes, twice:

1964: Bill White (1B), Charlie James (LF), and Ken Boyer (3B): April 19, 1964 vs. pitcher Bob Bruce of Houston (8th inning).

1985: Terry Pendleton (3B), Tom Nieto (C), and Brian Harper (PH): October 24, 1985 vs. pitcher Danny Jackson of the Royals (7th inning of World Series game 5).

FUN FACT: Over 130 years of MLB history, 75 pitchers have struck out 3 batters on 9 consecutive pitches (80 total occurrences). Sandy Koufax did it three times; Lefty Grove, Nolan Ryan, and Randy Johnson did it twice.

ISOLATED POWER (ISO):
MEASURES HITTER'S EXTRA BASES PER AT BAT

ISO FORMULA: SLUGGING % (SLG) MINUS BATTING AVERAGE (BA)
EXCELLENT (ABOVE .250), AVERAGE (.140), AWFUL (.080)

ISO Single Season (min. PA 400):

#1	Mark McGwire	.454	1998 (#4 in MLB)
#2	Mark McGwire	.418	1999
#3	Rogers Hornsby	.353	1925
#4	Jim Edmonds	.342	2003
#5	Jim Edmonds	.341	2004

FUN FACT: The #1 in a single-season ISO is Barry Bonds (Giants) with .536 in 2001; Babe Ruth (Yankees) is #2 with .473 in 1920. For career ISO (8000 PA), Babe Ruth is #1 with .348, and Barry Bonds is #2 with .309.

INNINGS PITCHED (IP) 300+
– SINGLE SEASON (SINCE 1920)

Rank	Player	Innings Pitched	Year
1	Dizzy Dean	325.1	1935 (28 wins/ERA 3.04)
2	Dizzy Dean	315.0	1936 (24 wins/ERA 3.17)
3	Bob Gibson	314.0	1969 (20 wins/ERA 2.18)
4	Dizzy Dean	311.2	1934 (30 wins/ERA 2.66)
5	Bob Gibson	304.2	1968 (22 wins/ERA 1.12)
6	Jesse Haines	301.2	1920 (13 wins/ERA 2.98)
7	Jesse Haines	300.2	1927 (24 wins/ERA 2.72)

FUN FACT: Wilbur Wood (White Sox) is #1 in MLB for most IP in a season with 376.2 in 1972; he went 24–17 that year with a 2.51 ERA and 8 shutouts.

JERSEYS

In the Cardinals' long history, only 14 jersey numbers (including non-number honorees Rogers Hornsby and Joe Buck) have been retired in honor of players, managers, broadcasters, and owners. Fittingly, the first was Stan Musial; the most recent was Tony La Russa. The Yankees are the only club having more retired numbers than the Cardinals with 20 numbers/21 individuals.

#1	Ozzie Smith SS*	1996
#2	Red Schoendienst 2B/Mgr*	1996
#6	Stan Musial LF*	1963
#9	Enos Slaughter RF*	1996
#10	Tony La Russa* Mgr	2012
#14	Ken Boyer 3B/Mgr	1984
#17	Dizzy Dean P*	1974
#20	Lou Brock LF*	1979

#24	Whitey Herzog Mgr*	2010
#42	Bruce Sutter P*	2004
#45	Bob Gibson P*	1975
#85	August Busch	1984
	Rogers Hornsby (no number)*	1997
	Jack Buck (announcer)*	2002

(* denotes HOF)

FUN FACT: Only one number, 42, is retired in all of baseball in honor of Jackie Robinson (1997). Per above, Cardinals pitcher Bruce Sutter also wore number 42.

Jerseys: Numbers – A Bit of History

Numbers on jerseys were first required by both MLB leagues in 1937. The first player to have his number retired was Yankee great Lou Gehrig (number 4) in 1939; the total now is over 150. The Yankees are the only team that retired the same number twice (number 8) for two great catchers: Bill Dickey and Yogi Berra. Interestingly, the number 7 (famed Yankee Mickey Mantle number) has only been retired twice; for Mantle and Craig Biggio (Astros).

Jerseys: Names Misspelled

The White Sox were the first to put names on jerseys and the first to misspell one for Ted Kluszewski (not an easy name): Kluszewsxi (with the 'Z' printed backwards). No Cardinals misspellings came up (welcome contributions) but here are some of the mistakes across MLB that appeared on the field:

"Natinals"	2009, Adam Dunn and Ryan Zimmerman
"San Francicso"	2010, Eugenio Velez
"Torotno"	1994, Joe Carter
"Cncinnati"	2005, Aaron Harang
"Angees"	2003, Adam Riggs

FUN FACT: Bill Veeck of the White Sox came up with the idea of putting names on jerseys in 1960. Ichiro Suzuki (Mariners) and Vida Blue (Giants) received special permission from MLB to use their first names on their jerseys. In 1969, Ken Harrelson (Indians) used his nickname, "Hawk." The Braves, at the urging of owner Ted Turner, tried nicknames in 1976 ("Knucksie" for Phil Niekro, etc.).

JULIAN "HOOLIE" JAVIER – CARDINALS 2B (1960–71)

A big impact player for the Cardinals (see highlights below), Julian Javier also played a major role in developing baseball in the Dominican Republic, his home country. He founded the Roberto Clemente League there, and in 1975 formed the Gigantes del Cibao, a notable competitor in the Dominican Winter Baseball League with his son Stan Javier, who also played in the majors.

Javier Career Highlights:

- Played 12 seasons with the Cardinals (final season with the Reds)

- Great defensive 2nd baseman, speedy base stealer

- Orlando Cepeda named him "The Phantom" for his smooth moves at 2nd base

- 19 World Series games for the Cards: batted .333 plus a 3-run home run

- All-Star in 1963 and 1968

- World Series champion in 1964 and 1967

- Sacrifice Hits (Bunts): # NL in 1966 with 15, #2 in 1962 and 1963 with 13

- Defensive Games as 2B: #1 NL with 161 in 1963

- Putouts as 2B: #1 NL in 1963 (377) and 1964 (360)

- Errors as 2B: #1 NL in 1960 (24) and 1964 (27)

- Cards career: .258/.297/.356 (BA/OBP/SLG)

FUN FACT: Osvaldo "Ozzie" Virgil Pichardo Sr. (IF) was the first Dominican to play in MLB; he debuted on September 23, 1956 for the Giants. There are two Cy Young winners from the Dominican Republic: Bartolo Colon (AL–2005) and Pedro Martinez (NL–1997, AL–1999 and 2000). Two Dominicans have been elected to the HOF: Juan Marichal (1983) and Pedro Martinez (2015).

JINXES AND SUPERSTITIONS (and Odd Routines)

Stan Musial

Stan ate the same breakfast every day during his 16-year career: an egg, then two pancakes, and then another egg.

Yadier Molina

Yadi had to kiss the gold catcher's mitt pendant on his necklace before each pitch.

Mark McGwire

McGwire reportedly wore his high school protective cup throughout his MLB career (16 years!).

Rogers Hornsby

Hornsby would not go to see "moving pictures" because the cinema experience might damage his vision.

Larry Walker

The former Cardinals outfielder was obsessed with the number 3. He set his alarm for 33 minutes after the hour, same with the microwave, he wore number 33, and got married on Nov 3rd at 3:33 p.m.

High Sock Sundays

Started by Daniel Descalso during the 2015 regular season inspired a winning streak for a period which even included Manager Mike Matheny.

Rally Squirrel

The squirrel is the "comeback mascot" which helped the Cards to win the World Series in 2011. It made its first appearance in Game 3 of the NLDS against the Phillies, and created a sensation when it ran right in front of Skip Schumaker at home plate. Reportedly, "happy flight" (Rafael Furcal's motivational chant) also helped the Cards win in 2011.

FUN FACT: Some other odd MLB superstitions (there are a lot)

- HOF Athletics second baseman Eddie Collins: kept gum on the on the top of his cap, and after getting two strikes at bat he would chew it again to prevent the third strike.

- HOF Pirate Willie Stargell of the Pirates (LF/1B): never hit using a bat with his name on it.

- HOF Giants Manager John McGraw: believed that a guy who showed up volunteering to try out for the team, and showed little baseball skill, was a good luck charm for the Giants through several seasons. Charles "Victory" Faust travelled with the team and McGraw let him pitch at the top of the ninth, and then Faust actually scored a run in the ninth (hit by pitch, stole second, then third, and scored).

- Mets/Cubs Relief Pitcher Turk Wendell: wore number 99 because Ricky "Wild Thing" Vaughn wore it in the movie Major League. He also brushed his teeth between innings, chewed 4 pieces of black licorice when he pitched, and took a big leap over the foul lines walking on/off the field. Wendell was named the most superstitious athlete of all time by Men's Fitness magazine.

- Legendary HOF Pitcher Satchel Paige: Satchel had his arm massaged with axle grease because it helped him pitch longer.

- HOF Red Sox third baseman Wade Boggs: Wade ended his pre-game practice by stepping on the bases in order (3rd, 2nd, 1st), stepping on the baseline (but stepping over it after the game started), and then took 2 steps in the coach's box, trotted to the dugout in exactly 4 steps, and so on.

- HOF Pirate shortstop Honus Wagner: Wagner concluded that his new automobile brought him bad luck when his batting average deteriorated so he stopped driving it.

K: STRIKEOUTS – CARDINALS PITCHERS

K: Strikeout Leaders (since 1900) – Single Season

Rank	Pitcher	Strikeouts	Year
1	Bob Gibson	274	1970
2	Bob Gibson	270	1965
3	Bob Gibson	269	1969
4	Bob Gibson	268	1968
5	Bob Gibson	245	1964

FUN FACT: The MLB leader in strikeouts (since 1900) is Nolan Ryan (RHP–Angels) with 383 in 1973. Bob Gibson is the Cardinals leader in career strikeouts with 3,117; Adam Wainwright (RHP) is second with 1,326 (through 2015). His 274 in 1970 is tied with Fergie Jenkins (Cubs 1970) and Mario Soto (Reds 1982).

K: Strikeout Leaders
(since 1900) – Career

#1	Bob Gibson	3,117	(IP 3884.1) (#14 in MLB)
#2	Adam Wainwright	1,487	(IP 1768.1)
#3	Dizzy Dean	1,095	(IP 1737.1)
#4	Chris Carpenter	1,085	(IP 1348.2)
#5	Bob Forsch	1,079	(IP 2658.2)

FUN FACT: Nolan Ryan RHP (Astros, etc.) holds the record for career strikeouts with 5,714; Randy Johnson LHP (Mariners, etc.) is second with 4,875 and Roger Clemens RHP ((Red Sox, etc.) third with 4,672.

K/9: Strikeouts Per 9 Innings – Single Season

Rank	Pitcher	Strikeouts	Year
1	Lance Lynn	8.84	2013 (IP 201.2)
2	Bob Gibson	8.39	1970 (IP 294.0)
3	Adam Wainwright	8.32	2010 (IP 230.1)
4	Jose DeLeon	8.31	1988 (IP 225.1)
5	Adam Wainwright	8.19	2009 (IP 233.0)

FUN FACT: Randy Johnson LHP (Diamondbacks) holds the single-season record with 13.41 in 2001; Pedro Martinez RHP (Red Sox) is second with 13.20. The career Cardinals leader is Lance Lynn with 8.71; the career MLB #1 is Randy Johnson with 10.61.

STRIKE THREE!

#1	Adam Wainwright	23.4%	2010
#2	Lance Lynn	23.1%	2013
#3	Bob Gibson	23.1%	1968
#4	Adam Wainwright	22.9%	2013
#5	Bob Gibson	22.6%	1970

FUN FACT: The #1 in MLB for K% in a single season is Pedro Martinez (Red Sox) with 37.5% in 1999.

K: Strikeout of FOUR Batters in ONE Inning (Bob Gibson):

On the Mound: Bob Gibson RHP

Behind the Plate: Tim McCarver C

June 7, 1966 (loss to the Pirates 9–1)

4th Inning:

Jerry Lynch: **Strikeout #1**

Jim Pagliaroni: **Strikeout #2**

Donn Clendenon: Walked. Steals second with Mazeroski at bat.

Bill Mazeroski: Swung at a wild pitch for **strikeout #3** and reached base safely.

(The catcher does not field the ball cleanly; instead of tagging the runner out, the runner reaches first. The strikeout is recorded and not the out.)

Don Cardwell: **Strikeout #4**

FUN FACT: Gibson is the only Cardinals pitcher to have a four-strikeout inning. According to baseball-almanac.com, there are 33 AL and 45 NL pitchers who have had a four-strikeout inning. The Dodgers pitchers have the most with 6; pitcher Chuck Finley had the most with three (twice with the Angels, once with the Indians).

K: STRIKEOUTS – BATTERS

K: Most Strikeouts – Single Season (400+ PA)

#1	Jim Edmonds (CF)	167	2000
			(#5 that year in MLB)
#2	Ron Gant (LF)	162	1997
#3	Mark McGwire (1B)	155	1998
#4	Matt Carpenter (3B)	151	2015
#5	Ray Lankford (LF)	150	1998

FUN FACT: The MLB #1 in single-season strikeouts is Mark Reynolds (1B Diamondbacks) with 223 in 2009; Adam Dunn is #2 with 222 in 2012 (1B White Sox). The career #1 in strikeouts is Reggie Jackson (RF Yankees) with 2,597. Lou Brock is #1 in career strikeouts for the Cardinals with 1,469.

K%: Strikeout Percentage/Highest – Single Season (400+ PA)

Rank	Player	K%	Year
1	Ray Lankford (LF)	31.4%	2000
2	Brandon Moss (1B/OF)	30.4%	2016
3	Randal Grichuk (OF)	29.5%	2016
4	Ron Gant (OF)	28.8%	1997
5	Chris Duncan (OF)	28.5%	2007

FUN FACT: The MLB #1 in K% is Melvin Nieves (OF Tigers) with 38.8% in 1997; his batting average was .228.

#1	Billy Southworth (OF)	9	1925
	Jimmy Brown (IF)	9	1938
#2	Frankie Frisch (2B)	10	1927
	Frankie Frisch (2B)	10	1934
	Andy High (3B)	10	1928

FUN FACT: The MLB #1 in fewest strikeouts is Joe Sewell (IF) with 3 in two seasons: 1930 (Indians – batting average .289) and 1932 (Yankees – batting average .272).

K%: Strikeout Percentage/Lowest – Single Season (400+ PA)

#1	Frankie Frisch (2B)	1.4%	1927
#2	Jimmie Brown (IF)	1.6%	1942
#3	Frankie Frisch (2B)	1.7%	1934
#4	Frankie Frisch (2B)	2.0%	1929
#5	Billy Southworth (OF)	2.1%	1926

FUN FACT: The #1 in MLB with the lowest K% is Joe Sewell (IF Yankees) with 0.5% in 1932; his batting average was .272.

K: Golden & Platinum Sombrero Cardinals (A Dubious Honor)

Golden Sombrero: 4 strikeouts in one game

Platinum Sombrero: 5 strikeouts in one game

Since 1952, Cardinals hitters have earned the Golden/Platinum Sombrero 100+ times, averaging about two times per season. Ray Lankford (CF) and Jim Edmonds (CF) are tied with seven total, but three of Lankford's are platinum while Edmonds are totally golden. Here are the leaders:

Golden Sombrero (4):

- Jim Edmonds (CF)   7
- Ryan Ludwick (OF)   5
- Lou Brock (LF)4
- Ray Lankford (CF)   4

Platinum Sombrero (5):

- Ray Lankford (CF)   3
- Dick Allen (IF) 1
- Steve Bilko   (1B)   1

FUN FACT: Ryan Howard (Phillies) is #1 (career) in MLB having 27 games with 4 or more strikeouts in his career. Reggie Jackson (Yankees) is #2 with 23, and Jim Thome (Indians/Phillies) is #3 with 20.

KNUCKLEBALL PITCHERS

What is a knuckleball: A pitch thrown to minimize the spin of the ball in flight, making it a challenging, erratic, unpredictable object coming at the batter. It is a pitch that travels slowly (50–70 mph), is difficult to throw, catch, or officiate (ball or strike?), and can be very successful when it works.

Knuckleball Cardinals – Jesse "Pop" Haines RHP:

Jesse "Pop" Haines made his Major League debut with the Reds, then managed by the legendary pitcher Christy Mathewson, in 1913. He was let go at the end of the year, and played in the minor leagues for some years. He debuted as a 26-year-old with the Cards in 1920 and in his first start pitched 12 scoreless innings before giving up 3 runs in the 13th for a Pirates win. Gaining the nickname of "Hard Luck Haines" with his fastball,

Jesse decided he needed something else and developed a knuckleball that "acted like a spitball," and things changed for the better (see stats below). He played for the Cards 18 consecutive seasons, and was the oldest in baseball when he retired at age 44 in 1937. His advice on how he lasted so long: "Get 8 hours of sleep a night, watch what you eat, lay off the alcohol, and throw the ball where you're looking."

1920–1937 Cardinals (HOF)

World Series championships: 1926, 1931, 1934

Five Pennants: Only Cardinal to play on the first five NL Pennant winning teams of 1926, 1928, 1930, 1931, and 1934.

20 game win seasons: 1923 (20), 1927 (24), 1928 (20)

No-hitter: July 17, 1924 vs. the Boston Braves

ERA: 3.64

ERA+: 109

SO (Strikeouts): 979

Win–Loss: 210–158

W–L %: .571

IP (Innings Pitched): 3,203.2

WHIP (Walks & Hits per IP): 1.350

CG (Complete Games): 209

SHO (Shutouts): 23

SO/W (Strikeout-to-Walk Ratio): 1.13

WP (Wild Pitches): 55

FIP (Field Independent Pitching): 3.96

Other Knuckleballers who played for the Cards:

- Al Papai RHP: 1948, 1950 – 23 games (ERA 5.14)
- Barney Schultz RHP: 1955, 1963–65 – 107 games (ERA 3.85)
- Hoyt Wilhelm RHP: 1957 (HOF) – 40 games (ERA 4.25)
- Bob Purkey RHP: 1965 – 32 games (ERA 5.79)
- Eddie Fisher RHP: 1973 – 6 games (ERA 1.29)

FUN FACT: Baseball historians point to either Toad Ramsey of the Louisville Colonels or Eddie Cicotte of the White (Black) Sox for inventing the knuckleball. Other famous knuckleballers include HOFers Ted Lyons (White Sox), Hoyt Wilhelm (Giants, etc.), and Phil Niekro (Braves). Niekro was the first knuckleballer to win 300 games. Other non-HOF knuckleballer standouts include Dutch Leonard (Senators) and Charlie Hough (Dodgers).

R.A. Dickey RHP (Blue Jays) stands out as a current knuckleball pitcher, and is the first one to win a Cy Young Award (2012), while pitching for the Mets.

In 2016, Dickey was scheduled to face another knuckleballer, Steven Wright (Red Sox), on April 9th, 2016, but thanks to a postponement it did not take place. The last time this happened was in 2000 when Tim Wakefield (Red Sox) pitched against Steve Sparks (Tigers); Red Sox won 7–6.

LOOGY: LEFT-HANDED ONE OUT GUY (PITCHER/RELIEF SPECIALIST)

Loogy Cardinals:

A LOOGY usually pitches fewer than 40 innings per season, going after one or maybe two high-leverage outs; here are a few:

- **Randy Choate** 2013–2015: 98.2 IP in 3 years with 82 strikeouts (196 games), 7.5 strikeouts per 9 innings (K/9), 3.56 ERA

- **Marc Rzepcynski** 2011–12, 2013: 79.2 IP in 3 years (109 games) with 70 strikeouts, 7.9 strikeouts per 9 innings (K/9), 4.63 ERA

- **Trever Miller** 2009–2010, 2011: 95.1 IP in 3 years (166 games) with 77 strikeouts, 7.3 strikeouts per 9 innings (K/9), 3.12 ERA

- **Steve Kline** 2001–04: 247.1 IP in 4 years (300 games) with 161 strikeouts, 5.9 strikeouts per 9 innings (K/9), 2.69 ERA

- *Jesse Orosco* 2000: 2.1 IP (6 games) with 4 strikeouts, 15.4 strikeouts per 9 innings (K/9), 3.86 ERA

- *Tony Fossas* 1995–97: 135.1 IP in 3 years (194 games) with 117 strikeouts, 7.8 strikeouts per 9 innings (K/9), 2.79 ERA

FUN FACT: Jesse Orosco LHP, who pitched briefly for the Cardinals in 2000 was a great example of a LOOGY. In the last five years of his career (Orioles, Dodgers, Cards, etc.), Orosco averaged less than a ½ IP per appearance. He pitched until age 46. One of the early LOOGY specialists was John "The Candy Man" Candelaria, who in 1991 averaged .571 innings in 59 games for the Dodgers.

LEFTIES: LEFT-HANDED STARTING & RELIEF PITCHERS

Lefties/Cardinals Pitchers (chronological)

- **Ted Breitenstein** (1892–1896, 1901): NL ERA leader 1893

- **Slim Sallee** (1908–16): #3 in ERA for Cardinals

- **Bill Sherdel** (1918–29, 1930, 1932): #1 in wins for Cardinals left-hander (153)

- **Max Lanier** (1938–46, 1949–51): NL ERA leader 1943

- **Harry Brecheen** (1940, 1943–52): MLB ERA leader 1948

- **Al Brazle** (1943–54): NL leader in saves 1952 & 1953

- **Howie Pollet** (1941–1950, 1951): 3-time All-Star

- **Steve Carlton** (1965–71): Struck out 19 Mets on 9/15/1969

- **Al Hrabosky** (1970–77): #3 Cy Young voting 1975 (22 saves)

- **John Tudor** (1985–87, 1988): #2 in Cy Young voting 1985 (10 shutouts)

- **Rick Ankiel** (1999–2001, 2004): #2 in Rookie of the Year voting 2000

More Recent CARDINALS Left-Handers:

- *Zach Duke* (2016–present)
- *Jaime Garcia* (2008–present)
- *Tyler Lyons* (2013–present)
- *Kevin Siegrist* (2013–present)

FUN FACT: The are 17 left-handed pitchers in the HOF as of 2016: Steve Carlton (former Cardinal), Andy Cooper (KC Monarchs), Whitey Ford (Yankee), Bill Foster (Chicago Giants), Tom Glavine (Braves), Lefty Gomez (Yankees), Lefty Grove (Athletics), Carl Hubbell (Giants), Randy Johnson (Mariners), Sandy Koufax (Dodgers), Rube Marquard (Giants), Hal Newhouser (Tigers), Herb Pennock (Yankees), Eddie Plank (Athletics), Eppa Rixey (Reds), Warren Spahn (Braves), Rube Waddell (Athletics).

LINEUPS: MOST OPENING DAY STARTS BY POSITION (1913–2016)

Whether or not a win on opening day predicts much about the coming season is open to question. The record for most consecutive Opening Day wins by a team is 9, shared by the Browns, Reds, and Mets. Nonetheless, Opening Day is eagerly anticipated every year and holds the promise, every year, of a great baseball season.

C	Yadier Molina	12	(2005–16)
	Ted Simmons	10	(1971–80)
	Del Rice	5	(1946, 1949, 1952–54)
	Darrell Porter	5	(1981–85)
1B	Jim Bottomley	10	(1923–32)
	Keith Hernandez	9	(1975–83)
	Albert Pujols	8	(2004–11)

2B	Julian Javier	11	(1961–71)
	Red Schoendienst	10	(1947–56)
	Frankie Frisch	9	(1927–29, 1931–36)
3B	Ken Boyer	11	(1955–1965)
	Ken Reitz	7	(1973–75, 1977–80)
	Terry Pendleton	6	(1985–1990)
SS	Ozzie Smith	13	(1982–88, 1990–95)
	Marty Marion	9	(1940–42, 1944–49)
	Edgar Renteria	6	(1999–2004)
LF	Lou Brock	14	(1965, 1967–79)
	Stan Musial	10	(1946, 1951–54, 1961)
	Matt Holliday	6	(2010–2015)
CF	Terry Moore	9	(1934–42)
	Curt Flood	8	(1962–69)
	Jim Edmonds	8	(2000–07)
RF	Enos Slaughter	10	(1938–42, 1946–47, 1951–53)
	Stan Musial	5	(1944, 48, 50, 56, 62)
	George Hendrick	5	(1980–84)
P	Bob Gibson	10	(1965, 1967–75)
	Dizzy Dean	5	(1933–37)
	Adam Wainwright	5	(2009, 2013–16)
	Chris Carpenter	5	(2005–07, 2010–11)
	Bob Forsch	4	(1978, 1981–83)

Lineups: Same Opening Day Lineup in 1967 and 1968

The Cardinals had the exact same starting lineup two years in a row in 1967 (April 11 win vs. the Giants) and 1968 (April 10 win vs. the Braves), including the same pitcher (the Dodgers have the most for position players opening day repeats with three years, 1977–79, but with two different pitchers):

C	Tim McCarver
1B	Orlando Cepeda
2B	Julian Javier
3B	Mike Shannon
SS	Dal Maxvill
LF	Lou Brock
CF	Curt Flood
RF	Roger Maris
P	Bob Gibson

FUN FACT: Hank Aaron (Braves) hit his 714th home run on opening day in 1974, to tie Babe Ruth (Yankees) on the all-time list. Senators pitching great Walter Johnson (Senators) threw a record 9 shutouts in his 14 season openers. The legendary Ted Williams (Red Sox) had a hit in every Opening Day game he appeared in (14). His Opening Day batting average was .449, with 3 home runs and 14 RBI.

LOB: LEFT ON BASE

LOB Base runner: the runner is LOB as of the end of the half-inning when he has not scored or been put out. It can be either a team or individual statistic. For the individual batter, it refers to the number of men remaining on base after that batter makes an out at the plate. For the team statistic, it is the number LOB at the end of an inning.

LOB: CARDINALS Team Stats

LOB Best – Single Season: 957 (1995)

- (MLB Record: Kansas City with 925 in 1957).

LOB Worst – Single Season: 1,251 (1939)

- (MLB Record: Browns with 1,334 in 1941).

LOB Worst – Single Game:

- The Cardinals tied the single game NL record mark with 18 LOB three times: vs. the Phillies on 9/15/28, Reds on 6/10/44, and Phillies on 9/14/50.

FUN FACT: The most LOB (20) occurred in the AL: Yankees vs. Reds on 9/21/56.

For individuals in a game, Ryan Zimmerman (Nationals) holds the record for 14 LOB in a 13-inning game on 5/8/16.

is for...

MUSIAL!
STAN "THE MAN" MUSIAL:

BASEBALL'S PERFECT WARRIOR,
BASEBALL'S PERFECT KNIGHT

Stan quote: "I love to play this game of baseball – I love putting on this uniform."

Carl Eskine P (Dodgers) on Stan: "I've had pretty good success throwing him my best pitch and backing up third."

Broadcaster Vin Scully on Stan: "How good was Stan Musial? He was good enough to take your breath away."

Musial Notes of Interest:

Nickname Origins: Reportedly the nickname "Stan the Man" was provided by admiring Brooklyn Dodgers fans who had great respect for Musial's prowess on the field: "Wow, he's the Man!"

Musial and Ken Griffey, Jr. were born on the same day—November 21—in different years, in the same town: Donora, Pennsylvania (Griffey Sr. was born there too). Besides athletes, Donora is famous for the Donora Smog of 1948, a tragic air inversion that trapped pollutants and killed 50 people, including Stan's father.

Musial signed as a pitcher with the Cardinals in 1938, had a 33–13 minor league record (ERA 3.52) with the Class D Williamson Colts and Daytona Beach Islanders before injuring his arm, and was converted to be an outfielder before making his debut on September 17, 1941.

Musial played the harmonica, including his rendition of "Take Me Out to the Ball Game" and performed on the T.V. show Hee Haw.

Stan owned Musial and Biggies Restaurant with businessman Julius "Biggie" Garagnani, which opened in 1949 on Chippewa and then moved to 5130 Oakland Avenue near Forest Park. A 1960s menu posted online included, of course, St. Louis favorite homemade toasted ravioli; the back cover advertises Stan and Biggie's hotel called "The Ivanhoe" in Miami Beach (100% air-conditioned!).

Musial received the Presidential Medal of Freedom from President Barack Obama in 2010 (the highest civilian honor for a U.S. citizen).

Stan Musial was never ejected from a game. In fact, he played the most games without an ejection (3,026); 2nd is Willie Mays (2,992) and 3rd is Brooks Robinson (2,896).

At retirement, Musial held MLB career records for extra base hits (XBH) and total bases (TB); and NL records for runs (R), hits (H), doubles (2B), and runs batted in (RBI).

Musial Won the 1955 All-Star game with a 12th inning walk-off homer; tied with Willie Mays for most All-Star Game appearances with 24.

Musial Served as General Manager for the Cardinals when they won the 1967 World Series over the Red Sox.

Musial is the only player in history to finish top ten in the NL for both batting average and home runs in 12 seasons. He hit above .300 for his first 17 seasons. He had 10 seasons with more than 100 RBI. He is also the only player in MLB to be in the top 30 for career batting numbers across the board.

Musial Ranking in the NL:
12 Seasons Top Ten in BA and HR:

Year	BA (Rank in NL)	HR (Rank in NL)
1943	.357 (#1)	13 (#6)
1946	.365 (#1)	16 (#5)
1947	.376 (#5)	19 (#10)
1948	.376 (#1)	39 (#3)
1949	.338 (#2)	36 (#2)
1950	.346 (#1)	28 (#8)
1951	.355 (#1)	32 (#4)
1952	.336 (#1)	21 (#8)
1953	.337 (#3)	30 (#7)
1954	.330 (#4)	35 (#7)
1955	.319 (#3)	33 (#7)
1957	.351 (#1)	29 (#7)

Musial Top Career Numbers (# in MLB):

Total Bases (TB):	6,134 (#2)
Extra Base Hits (XBH):	1,377 (#2)
Runs Created (RC):	2,562 (#3)
Doubles (2B):	725 (#3)
Hits (H):	3,630 (#4)
Runs Batted In (RBI):	1,951 (#5)
Home Runs (HR):	475 (#30)
Batting Average (BA):	.331 (#30)

Musial Poem: The Tycoon by Ogden Nash

The business life of Mr. Musial
is, to say the least, unusual.
First base, outfield, restaurant, bank,
All are home to Stanley Frank.
One moment, slugger of lethal liners,
The next, mine host to hungry diners,
And, between the slugging and the greeting,
To the bank for the director's meeting.
Yet no one grudges success to Stan,
Good Citizen and family man,
Though I would love to have his job –
One half tycoon, one half Ty Cobb.

Source: (Life, September 5, 1955)

MINOR LEAGUES

Minor League Cardinals Affiliates (High-A to AAA)

- Memphis Redbirds (AAA) – Pacific Coast League

- Springfield Cardinals (AA) – Texas League

- Palm Beach (High-A) – Florida State League

FUN FACT: How much do they make? According to an August 2016 article, the starting salary for a first-year player in the minor leagues at the class A level is about $1,100 per month. Most minor leaguers make less than $10,000 per season. More than 80 percent of those players will never reach the big leagues. If they do, the pay-off is good: the average major league player salary in 2016 is about $4.4 million per year. (Washington Post, 08/28/16, "It's Not-Much-Money Ball" by Kent Babb and Jorge Castillo)

Minor Leagues – Notable Cardinals PLAYER/PITCHER of the Year Awards

Minor League PLAYER OF THE YEAR

- **1996**   Dmitri Young IF
- **2000**   Albert Pujols 3B
- **2010**   Matt Carpenter 3B
- **2011**   Matt Adams 1B
- **2013**   Kolten Wong 2B
- **2015**   Stephen Piscotty OF

Minor League PITCHER OF THE YEAR

- **1998**   Rick Ankiel LHP
- **2003**   Dan Haren RHP

- **2009**   Lance Lynn RHP
- **2010**   Shelby Miller RHP
- **2011**   Shelby Miller RHP
- **2015**   Alex Reyes RHP and Austin Gomber LHP (co-winners)

FUN FACT: Drafted number 72 by the Cardinals in 1997, LHP Rick Ankiel received a $2.5 million signing bonus, then one of the highest ever received. The number one pick that year (Matt Anderson, RHP, Tigers) received only a bit more at $2,505,000. Ankiel got off to a great start with the Cardinals, but then became famous for throwing wild pitches during game one division series against the Braves, including five in one inning. He successfully converted to being a position player, ending with the Mets in 2013. Recent signing bonuses:

MANAGERS

Managers: Cardinals Managers of the Year Winners (Wins–Losses)

- **1985**   Whitey Herzog   101–61
- **2002**   Tony La Russa   97–65

Managers: HALL OF FAME (HOF) – By # OF CARDINALS Wins

(* denotes managers elected to the HOF as players)

1.	Tony La Russa	1,408	(2,591 games)	1996–2011
2.	Red Schoendienst*	1,041	(1,999 games)	1965–76, 1980, 1990
3.	Whitey Herzog	822	(1,553 games)	1980–90

4.	Billy Southworth	620	(981 games)	1929, 1940–45
5.	Branch Rickey	458	(947 games)	1919–25
	Frankie Frisch*	458	(822 games)	1933–38
6.	Joe Torre	351	(706 games)	1990–95
7.	Miller Huggins	346	(774 games)	1913–17
8.	Roger Bresnahan*	255	(607 games)	1909–12
9.	Bill McKechnie	129	(217 games)	1928–29
10.	Kid Nichols*	80	(168 games)	1904–05
11.	Roger Connor*	8	(45 games)	1896 (Browns)

FUN FACT: Roger Connor holds the lowest winning percentage in Cardinals manager history, with .178; he was a better player and is known for holding the record for career home runs (138) before Babe Ruth took over. The highest winning percentage is held by Billy Southworth with .642. Tony La Russa, with 2,728 career wins, is #3 on the MLB list of all-time wins by a manager; Connie Mack (Athletics) is #1 with 3,731, and John McGraw (Giants) is #2 with 2,728.

Managers: 100-plus Wins in a Season – Wins (Winning %)

*won the World Series

#1	1942	Billy Southworth*	106 wins (.688)
#2	2004	Tony La Russa*	105 wins (.617)
	1944	Billy Southworth*	105 wins (.682)
	1943	Billy Southworth	105 wins (.682)
#3	1985	Whitey Herzog*	101 wins (.620)
	1967	Red Schoendienst*	101 wins (.627)
	1931	Gabby Street*	101 wins (.656)
#4	2015	Mike Matheny	100 wins (.617)
	2005	Tony La Russa*	100 wins (.617)

FUN FACT: Billy Southworth ranks #1 thru #3 in single-season Winning Percentage (%): 1942 (.688), 1943 (.682), and 1944 (.682). Gabby Street is next with .656 in 1931. As for the most wins in one season, the 1906 Cubs are tied with the 2001 Mariners with 116. Results? The 1906 Cubs under manager Frank Chance lost the World Series to the White Sox; the 2001 Mariners led by Lou Piniella lost in the ALCS to the Yankees.

Managers/HOF: Some Notes on Cardinals HOF Managers (Chronological)

Connor (1895): Roger Connor (1B) was a player-manager during part of his second season with the St. Louis Browns (NL) in 1895, and remained until 1897 when he retired, putting up a .304 batting average during his time at St. Louis. Connor was the first power hitter in MLB, hitting 138 career home runs which he lived to see surpassed by Babe Ruth in 1921. He topped .300 for 11 seasons and hit the first NL grand slam home run on Sept 10, 1881. As a Giant in 1886, he hit such a huge home run out of the Polo Grounds that members of the New York Stock Exchange, impressed with the feat, collected money to fund a $500 gold watch that was presented to him a few days later.

Nichols (1904–05): Charles "Kid" Nichols was a pitcher who played for Boston (1890–1901), and then a player-manager for the CARDS (1904–05); he closed off as a pitcher with the Phillies (1905–06). In St. Louis, Nichols went 22–18, with 3 shutouts and a 1.085 WHIP. He is the youngest player in MLB history to join the 300 WIN club. He won 20 or more games in his first 10 seasons, thanks mostly to his fastball.

Bresnahan (1909–12): Roger Bresnahan started out as a pitcher, making his debut with the Washington Senators in 1897. He was a catcher with John Mcgraw's Giants from 1902–1908, and made history on opening day 1907 when he experimented with wearing protective gear (shin guards), and tried out a batting helmet. Fans reacted negatively, and umpire Bill Klem had to call off the game. Bresnahan was elected as a player to the HOF. In the 1905 World Series, he hit .313 in the Giants win over the Athletics.

Huggins (1913–17): Miller Huggins (2B) played with the Cards from 1910–16. He set an MLB record in 1910 for 6 plate appearances

(PA) with no at-bats (AB) because of 4 walks and 2 sacrifice flies. He succeeded Roger Bresnahan as Cards manager in 1913 because the Cards owner, Helene Hathaway Britton, "preferred his 'gentlemanly' ways" (Bresnahan was the one who said a woman could not run a baseball team). Huggins left the Cards to manage the Yankees, including the Murderer's Row team of the 1920s that won six AL pennants and three World Series.

Rickey (1919–25): Branch Rickey ("The Mahatma") was a catcher before becoming famous for revolutionizing baseball with the Cards (started the "farm" system in place now) and integrating baseball with the signing of Jackie Robinson for the Dodgers (for more on Rickey, see "V" for visionary in this book). His best year as a Cards manager was in 1921 with an 87–66 record; 1922 was also a good year (85–69) with attendance spiking to a record 536,343.

Mckechnie (1928–29): Bill McKechnie (3B) made his debut in 1907 for the Pirates, and managed the Cards 1928–29. He had the nickname of "Deacon" because he sang in his church choir. He was a very religious man (like Branch Rickey), and did not drink, smoke, or use profanity. McKechnie is currently #13 on the MLB manager wins list with 1,896 (an overall .524 win percentage). He was Manager of the Year in 1937 (Boston Braves) and 1940 (Reds), and was the first manager to win pennants with three different NL teams: Pirates (1925), Cards (1928), and Reds (1939 and 1940).

Street (1929–1933): Gabby Street was part of a famous stunt, when he was a catcher for the Washington Senators, for catching a baseball dropped from the Washington Monument (555 feet). He was also the catcher/mentor for the legendary pitcher, Walter Johnson. Street managed for the Browns in 1938, and became a color commentator for Cards and Browns radio broadcasts after WWII, working with Harry Caray.

Frisch (1933–38): Frankie Frisch (2B) was traded to the Cards in 1926 for Rogers Hornsby. He is #1 on the switch hitter list for career batting average with .316. He is one of two players to hit .300 from both sides of the plate; Chipper Jones (3B Braves) was the other. Frisch became the player-manager of the Cards in 1933, and was in charge of the 1934 "Gashouse Gang" Cardinals, which included seven future Hall of Famers, and went on to win the World Series. He is tied with Branch Rickey for franchise wins with 458. "The Fordham Flash" was elected to the HOF as a player, juggling manager and 2B responsibilities for six seasons. Frisch was a 3-time All-Star (1933–35), 3-time NL stolen base leader, and NL MVP in 1931.

Southworth (1929, 1940–45): Billy Southworth (OF) debuted with the Indians in 1913, and played for the World Series Champion Giants in 1926, batting .320 with 99 RBI and 16 home runs during the regular season that year. Joining the CARDS in 1929, Southworth was not very popular (or successful) when he tried managing, lasting only until July 21 when he was fired. Reportedly, he overdid trying to impose discipline, trying to ban the players from using their automobiles and conducting constant curfew checks. Things changed a decade later when Southworth returned to manage the Cards in 1940, and ended up #4 in franchise wins (620). Over six full seasons, "Billy the Kid" averaged 101 wins from 1941–45, won three pennants, and two World Series championships in 1942 and 1944. He went on to manage the Boston Braves (1946–51), and his overall career winning percentage of .597 places him at #5 on the all-time list.

Schoendienst (1965–76): Red Schoendienst (2B) debuted with the CARDS in 1945, and returned to make his last MLB appearance with them in 1963. He has the second-longest tenure as a manager behind Tony La Russa, and second to him in wins (1,041). He was elected to the HOF in 1989 as a player, and stands out as someone who was successful both in the field and as a coach/manager. As of 2016, he is still with the Cards as a special assistant coach, meaning he has spent 71 years in MLB (see "S" for more on Schoendienst's career).

Herzog (1980–90): Whitey (born Dorrell) Herzog, a lefty outfielder (OF), debuted with the Washington Senators in 1956, and finished off with the Tigers in 1963. As a manager, he became known for "Whitey Ball," featuring aggressive base running, excellence in defense, and a strong bullpen. Upon arrival in St. Louis in 1980, he made a splash with three trades involving 21 players. Herzog won three NL pennants (1982,

1985, and 1987) and the 1982 World Series; he is #3 in franchise wins (822). In his eight full seasons with the Cards, attendance exploded, drawing at least 2.4 million fans per year, and more than 3 million for the first two times in Cards history (1987 and 1989).

Torre (1990–95): Joe Torre played for the Cards from 1969–74, initially replacing Orlando "Cha Cha" Cepeda at 1B. With the trade of Tim McCarver (C) in 1970, Torre spent time at catcher and 3B. In 1971, he won the NL MVP, and was the League leader in batting average and RBI. Torre managed first with the Mets and the Braves, and then replaced Cards Manager Whitey Herzog in 1990. His best record was in 1993 with 87–75. As manager of the Yankees (1996–2007), Torre won four World Series championships. He is #5 on the all-time manager wins list with 2,326 (.538 win percentage).

La Russa (1996–2011): Tony La Russa, former infielder (IF) for the Athletics, Braves, and Cubs, became a manager in 1979 for the White Sox. He earned his law degree and passed the Florida Bar in 1980, joining a short list of MLB managers with the same qualifications, including some other Cards managers: Branch Rickey, Jack Hendricks, and Miller Huggins. La Russa is the winningest Cardinals manager in franchise history (1,408 wins), and is just one of two managers to win a world championship in both leagues (Sparky Anderson is the other). La Russa is #3 on the all-time manager wins list with 2,278, after Connie Mack (3,731), and John McGraw (2,763).

FUN FACT: – Notes On Other Cardinals Managers:

Von der Ahe (1892): Chris Von der Ahe was the owner/manager of the Browns at a difficult time. He tried to attract fans by surrounding the ballpark with an amusement park dubbed "Coney Island West" and brought him the nickname of "Von Der Ha Ha." His record: 56–94.

Blades (1939–40): Ray Blades was a tough competitor and, while it is unknown whether banning player consumption of alcohol helped, he was able to get 92 wins his first season with the Cards, taking them from 6th to 2nd place in the NL. Things did not go so well in 1940, and Blades was fired and replaced by Billy Southworth.

Dyer (1946–50): Eddie Dyer, in his first season, led the Cards to the first postseason playoff in MLB history, going on to beat the Red Sox for the 1946 World Championship. Dyer ranks 7th in franchise history with 446 wins. In his playing career with the Cards from 1922–27, Dyer played outfield, 1st base, and pitched, and then switched to managing in the Cardinal farm system in 1928.

Stanky (1952–55): Eddie Stanky, as a player (2B), became known for the "Stanky Maneuver," distracting opposing hitters by jumping up and down, waving his hands around. As the Cards player-manager, Stanky was good at holding up games close to being called for darkness when it worked to the Cards' benefit (walking slowly to the mound after every pitch to confer), resulting in the MLB one-trip-per-inning rule. He was Manager of the Year in 1952.

Keane (1961–64): Johnny Keane led the Cards to an unexpected World Series Championship over the Yankees in 1964, the first since 1946. The season had not been going well and most of the front office executives were fired in August as a "house cleaning." Keane survived, and the NL-leading Phillies melted down enough for the Cards to move on. After the World Series win, Keane surprised everyone by resigning and was replaced by Red Schoendienst.

Matheny (2012–Present): Mike Matheny, as a catcher for the Cardinals (2000–04), helped St. Louis reach the postseason four of his five years with his defensive and leadership contributions, winning three of his four Gold Gloves. As a manager beginning in 2012, Matheny has a number of accomplishments: first MLB manager to take his team to the playoffs in his first four seasons (2012–15), has a 100-win season (2015), and was the NL manager in the 2014 All-Star game.

N is for...

NICKNAMES: NOTABLE CARDINALS NAMES

- **"Stan the Man"** Stan Musial (OF/1B)

- **"The Wizard of Oz"** Ozzie Smith (SS)

- **"Red"** Albert Schoendienst (2B/Mgr)

- **"Whitey"** Dorrel Herzog (Mgr)

- **"The Raja"** Rogers Hornsby (2B)

- **"Gibby"** and **"Hoot"** Bob Gibson (P)

- **"Country"** Enos Slaughter (RF)

- **"The Mad Hungarian"** Al Hrabosky (P)

- **"Big Mac"** Mark McGwire (1B)

- **"Dizzy"** and **"Daffy"** Jay (P) and Paul Dean (P)

- **"The Big Cat"** and **"Big Jawn"** Johnny Mize (1B)

- **"Ducky"** Joe Medwick (LF)

the **WIZARD OF OZ**

- **"Gashouse Gang"** 1930's Cardinals (1934 World Series Champions)

- **"Pepper"** Johnny Martin (OF/3B)

- **"Fordham Flash"** Frankie Frisch (2B)

- **"Wild Bill"** Bill Hallahan (P)

- **"Sunny Jim"** Jim Bottomley (1B)

- **"Spud"** Virgil Davis (C)

- **"Leo the Lip"** Leo Durocher (SS)

- **"Bake"** Arnold McBride (CF)

- **"Lefty"** Steve Carlton (P)

- **"Creepy"** Joe Crespi (2B)

- **"Specs"** George Toperczer (IF)

- **"Base Burglar"** Lou Brock (LF)

- **"Silent"** George Hendrick (OF)

- **"Zamboni"** Ken Reitz (3B)

- **"Buttermilk Tommy"** Tommy Dowd (OF/2B)

- **"Sure Shot"** Fred Dunlap (2B)

- **"Ripper"** James Collins (1B)

- **"Pop"** Jesse Haines (P)

- **"Jumpsteady"** Garry Templeton (SS)

- **"Scrabble"** Mark Rzepczysnki (P)

- **"The Final Boss"** Seung-Hwan Oh (P/Closer)

FUN FACT: There are so many great baseball nicknames. A few of the notable ones include: "Charlie Hustle" (Pete Rose), "Kung Fu Panda" (Pablo Sandoval), "Donnie Baseball" (Don Mattingly), "The Splendid Splinter" (Ted Williams), "The Commerce Comet" (Mickey Mantle), and "The Sultan of Swat (Babe Ruth).

NATIONAL LEAGUE (NL) MVP Award Winners – CARDINALS

NL MVP – Cardinals Leaders

3 times – Stan Musial (1943, 1946, 1948)

3 times – Albert Pujols (2005, 2008, 2009)

- Only pitchers: Bob Gibson (1968), Dizzy Dean (1945), and Mort Cooper (1942)

FUN FACT: Musial was the first NL player to win three MVPs; in his last MVP season, 1948, Musial missed the Triple Crown by one home run.

NL MVP winners (1924–29 was the League Award, first MVP in 1931):

1925	Rogers Hornsby 2B (Triple Crown year)
1926	Bob O'Farrell C
1928	Jim Bottomley 1B
1931	Frankie Frisch 2B
1934	Dizzy Dean P
1937	Joe Medwick LF (Triple Crown year)
1942	Mort Cooper P
1943	Stan Musial OF
1944	Marty Marion SS
1946	Stan Musial 1B
1948	Stan Musial OF
1964	Ken Boyer 3B

1967	Orlando Cepeda 1B
1968	Bob Gibson RHP
1971	Joe Torre 3B
1979	Keith Hernandez 1B (tied with Willie Stargell)
1985	Willie McGee OF
2005	Albert Pujols 1B
2008	Albert Pujols 1B
2009	Albert Pujols 1B

FUN FACT: First basemen have won the most MVPs. Four teams have never had an MVP winner: Diamondbacks, Marlins, Mets, and Rays (through 2015). Barry Bonds (LF–Pirates/Giants) has won the most MVPs with 7.

NATIONAL LEAGUE (NL) CENTRAL

National League (NL) History:

The NL "Classic Eight" team was the NL lineup established in 1900, remaining unchanged through 1952:

Boston Beaneaters/now Atlanta Braves

Brooklyn Superbas/now Los Angeles Dodgers

Chicago Orphans/now Chicago Cubs

Cincinnati Reds

New York Giants/now San Francisco Giants

Philadelphia Phillies

Pittsburgh Pirates

St. Louis Cardinals

NL Expansion and Change:

- **1962:** Added New York Mets and Houston Colt .45's – 10 teams

- **1969:** Added San Diego Padres and Montreal Expos – 12 teams

- **1969:** NL divided into two divisions – East and West

- **1993:** Added Colorado Rockies and Florida Marlins – 14 teams

- **1994:** NL reorganized to three divisions (East, Central, West)

- **1998:** Added Arizona Diamondbacks – 15 teams

- Milwaukee Brewers move from AL to NL – 16 teams

- **2013:** Houston moves to AL West – back to 15 teams

NL Central History:

- **1994:** Creation of NL Central

- Reds and Astros – from the NL West

- Cardinals, Cubs, and Pirates – from the NL East

- **1998:** Brewers moved in from American League (AL) Central, making the NL Central the largest division in baseball.

- **2013:** Astros moved out to the American League (AL) West.

- **2016:** Cardinals, Cubs, Pirates, Reds, Brewers

FUN FACT: The Pirates have made several attempts to move back to the NL East. They have not won the division since it was created in 1994, but have three wild card wins. The division has been dominated by the Cardinals: 21 division championships and three wild card wins.

NL Central Teams:
World Series Wins (Years):

#1	Cardinals	11	(1926, 31, 34, 42, 44, 46, 64, 67, 82, 2006, 2011)
#2	Pirates	5	(1909, 25, 60, 71, 79)
	Reds	5	(1919, 40, 75, 76, 90)
#3	Cubs	2	(1907, 08)
#4	Brewers	1	(1957)

FUN FACT: Until 1997, AL and NL teams met each other only in the World Series (or in exhibition games). Beginning in '97, interleague games started during the regular season and were counted in the standings. In 1999, AL and NL presidents were discontinued and umpires were united under MLB (not league) control. As of 2011, interleague games took place throughout the season. The major difference between the two leagues is the AL's adoption of the designated hitter (DH) in 1973, with the DH batting in place of the pitcher. During the regular season, the home team determines whether the DH is used; for spring training, it varies but is up to the manager's discretion. In the minor leagues at AA and AAA, the DH is used unless both teams are NL; Class A or lower, the DH is always used.

is for...

OBP: ON-BASE PERCENTAGE

FORMULA: (Hits + Walks + Hit-by-Pitch) divided by (At Bats + Walks + Hit-by-Pitch + Sac Flies)

OBP: Cardinals – Career Leaders (PA: min 3,500 plate appearances)

#1	Rogers Hornsby 2B	.427	(6,716)
#2	Albert Pujols 1B	.420	(7,433)
#3	Johnny Mize 1B	.419	(3,581)
#4	Stan Musial OF/1B	.417	(12,718)
#5	Jim Edmonds OF	.393	(4,356)
#6	Jim Bottomley 1B	.387	(6,008)
#7	Keith Hernandez 1B	.385	(4,724)
#8	Enos Slaughter OF	.384	(7,710)
#9	Joe Torre C/1B	.382	(3,909)
#10	Matt Holliday OF	.380	(4,121)

FUN FACT: Cardinal Jesse Burkett LF (1899–1901) had a .444 OBP, but only 1,951 plate appearances. Ted Williams LF (Red Sox) is #1 in MLB for OBP with .482

OBP: Cardinals – Single-Season Leaders (min 500 PA)

Rank	Player	OBP (Year)
1	Rogers Hornsby 2B	.507 (1924)
2	Rogers Hornsby 2B	.490 (1925)
3	Mark McGwire 1B	.482 (1998)
4	Albert Pujols 1B	.470 (2008)
5	Jack Clark RF	.459 (1987)
5	Rogers Hornsby 2B	.459 (1922)
6	Rogers Hornsby 2B	.458 (1921)
7	Joe Cunningham 1B	.453 (1959)
8	Stan Musial OF/1B	.450 (1944)
9	Stan Musial OF/1B	.449 (1951)
10	Johnny Mize 1B	.444 (1930)

FUN FACT: Barry Bonds LF (Giants) has the highest single-season OBP with .609 in 2004.

OPS: THE "S" PORTION – SLUGGING PERCENTAGE

Slugging Percentage Formula: TB (Total Bases) divided by AB (At Bats)

Slugging Percentage – Career Leaders (min 3,500 PA)

#1	Albert Pujols 1B	.617
#2	Johnny Mize 1B	.600
#3	Rogers Hornsby 2B	.568

#4	Stan Musial 1B/OF	.559
#5	Jim Edmonds OF	.555
#6	Joe Medwick OF	.545
#7	Jim Bottomley 1B	.537
#8	Matt Holliday OF	.494
#9	Ray Lankford OF	.481

FUN FACT: The #1 in career slugging percentage is Babe Ruth (Yankees) with .690; Ted Williams (Red Sox) is #2 with .634; and Lou GEHRIG (Yankees) is #3 with .632.

Slugging Percentage – Single-Season Leaders (min 500 PA)

#1	Rogers Hornsby 2B	.756	1925
#2	Mark McGwire 1B	.752	1998
#3	Rogers Hornsby 2B	.722	1922
#4	Stan Musial 1B/OF	.702	1948
#5	Mark McGwire 1B	.697	1999
#6	Rogers Hornsby 2B	.696	1924
#7	Albert Pujols 1B	.671	2006
#8	Albert Pujols 1B	.667	2003
#9	Albert Pujols 1B	.658	2009
#10	Albert Pujols 1B	.657	2004

FUN FACT: The #1 in single-season slugging percentage is Barry Bonds (Giants) with .863 in 2001; #2 is Babe Ruth (Yankees) with .849 in 1920, and #3 is Babe Ruth (Yankees) with .846 in 1921.

OPS: ON-BASE PLUS SLUGGING PERCENTAGE

OPS Formula: Add OBP (see above) and Slugging Percentage (SLG)

OPS: Career Leaders (min 3,500 PA)

#1	*Albert Pujols 1B*	*1.037*
#2	Johnny Mize 1B	1.018
#3	Rogers Hornsby 2B	.995
#4	Stan Musial 1B/OF	.976
#5	Jim Edmonds OF	.947
#6	Jim Bottomley 1B	.924
#7	Joe Medwick OF	.917
#8	Matt Holliday OF	.874
#9	Enos Slaughter 1B	.847
#10	Ray Lankford OF	.846

FUN FACT: The MLB #1 in career OPS is Babe Ruth OF (Yankees) with 1.164, who is also #1 in SLG with .690. Per above, the #1 in the other part of the OPS equation, OBP, is Ted Williams.

OPS: Single Season Leaders (BA – batting average)

Rank	Player	OPS	BA	Year
1	Rogers Hornsby 2B	1.245	.405	1925
2	Mark McGwire 1B	1.222	.299	1998
3	Rogers Hornsby 2B	1.203	.424	1924
4	Rogers Hornsby 2B	1.181	.401	1922

Rank	Player	OPS	BA	Year
5	Stan Musial 1B/OF	1.152	.376	1948
6	Mark McGwire 1B	1.120	.278	1999
7	Albert Pujols 1B	1.114	.357	2008
8	Albert Pujols 1B	1.106	.359	2003
9	Albert Pujols 1B	1.102	.331	2006
10	Albert Pujols 1B	1.101	.327	2009

FUN FACT: The #1 in single-season OPS is Barry Bonds LF (Giants) with 1.422 (his SLG was .812) in 2004; he is also the #1 in single season SLG with .863 in 2001.

OFFENSE: CARDINALS LEADERS BY POSITION – SINGLE SEASON

Offense by Position: Most Home Runs (HR)

POS	PLAYER	YEAR	HR
C	Ted Simmons	1979	26
1B	Mark McGwire	1998	69
2B	Rogers Hornsby	1922	42
SS	Jhonny Peralta	2014	21
3B	Fernando Tatis	1999	34
	Scott Rolen	2004	34
LF	Stan Musial	1951	32
CF	Jim Edmonds	2000	41
RF	Stan Musial	1948	39
P	Bob Gibson	1965	5
	Bob Gibson	1972	5

Offense by Position:
Most Runs Batted In (RBI)

C	Ted Simmons	1972	96
1B	Mark McGwire	1999	147
2B	Rogers Hornsby	1922	152
SS	Edgar Rentaria	2003	100
3B	Joe Torre	1971	137
LF	Joe Medwick	1937	154
CF	Jim Edmonds	2001	110
RF	Stan Musial	1948	131
P	Dizzy Dean	1935	21

Offense by Position:
Most Stolen Bases (SB)

C	Yadier Molina	2012	12
1B	Gregg Jefferies	1993	46
2B	Delino DeShields	1997	54
SS	Ozzie Smith	1988	57
3B	Pepper Martin	1933	26
LF	Lou Brock	1974	118
CF	Willie McGee	1985	56
RF	Andy Van Slyke	1985	33
P	Bob Gibson	1969	5

FUN FACT: In fangraphs.com, you can sort through by position/year/ stat to see who ranked where at each position. For example, Vern Stephens (Red Sox) has the most RBI at SS since 1930 with 159 in 1949; Lou Gehrig (Yankees) has the most RBI at 1B with 184 in 1932; and Davey Lopes (Dodgers – now 1B coach with the Nationals) has the most SB with 77 in 1975.

Base BURGLAR

is for...

GIBSON

PITCHERS: GAMES — STARTED, SAVES (SINCE 1920)

Pitchers: Most Games Started (Innings Pitched/IP) — Career

#1	Bob Gibson RHP	482	(3884.1 IP)
#2	Bob Forsch RHP	401	(2658.2 IP)
#3	Jesse Haines RHP	388	(3203.2 IP)
#4	Bill Doak RHP	319	(2387.0 IP)
#5	Adam Wainwright RHP	242	(1756.2 IP – active player)
#6	Bill Sherdel LHP	242	(2450.2 IP)
#7	Harry Brecheen LHP	224	(1790.1 IP)
#8	Ted Breitenstein LHP	220	(1896.2 IP)
#9	Slim Sallee LHP	215	(1905.1 IP)
#10	Larry Jackson RHP	209	(1672.1 IP)

FUN FACT: The #1 in MLB for games started is Cy Young (Cleveland, former Cardinal) with 815, #2 is Nolan Ryan (Astros, etc.) with 773, and #3 is Don Sutton (Dodgers) with 756.

Pitchers: Most Games STARTED (Innings Pitched/IP) – Single Season

#1	*Joaquin Andujar RHP*	38	(269.2)	1985
	Larry Jackson RHP	38	(282.0)	1960
#2	Joaquin Andujar RHP	37	(265.2)	1982
	Bill Doak RHP	37	(270.0)	1920
	Jesse Haines RHP	37	(301.2)	1920
	Larry Jackson RHP	37	(256.0)	1959
	Ferdie Schupp LHP	37	(250.2)	1920

FUN FACT: The #1 in games started is Wilbur Wood (White Sox) with 49 in 1973; he is also #2 with 48 in 1973; #3 is Mickey Lolich (Tigers) with 45 in 1971.

PITCHERS: WINS, WINS%, BAA (since 1900)

(Additional Pitcher Stats under "K" and "W" – see index in the back)

Pitchers: WINS (W) – Career Leaders

Rank	Pitcher	Career Wins
1	Bob Gibson RHP	251
2	Jesse Haines RHP	210
3	Bob Forsch RHP	163
4	Bill Sherdel LHP	153
5	Bill Doak RHP	144
6	Adam Wainwright RHP	134 – active player
6	Dizzy Dean RHP	134
7	Harry Brecheen LHP	128

FUN FACT: The career WINS leader in MLB is Cy Young (various teams including Cardinals for 2 years) with 511, probably an unbeatable record. #2 is Walter Johnson (Senators) with 417, and tied at #3 with 373 are Grover Cleveland "Pete" Alexander (hero of the Cardinals 1926 World Series) and Christy Mathewson (Giants).

Pitchers: WINS (W) – Single- Season Leaders

#1	**Dizzy Dean RHP**	**30**	**1934**
#2	Dizzy Dean RHP	28	1935
#3	Ted Breitenstein LHP	27	1894
#4	Cy Young RHP	26	1899
#5	Dizzy Dean RHP	24	1936
	Jesse Haines RHP	24	1927
#6	Bob Gibson RHP	23	1970

FUN FACT: The pitcher with the most wins single season is Old Hoss Radbourn (RHP–Providence Grays) with 59 in 1884; since 1900, Jack Chesbro (RHP–Highlanders) had the most with 41 in 1904.

Pitchers: Winning Percentage (%) – Single-Season Leaders (win–loss record)

Rank	Pitcher	Winning %	Year	Record
1	Kyle Lohse RHP	.842	2012	16–3
2	Dizzy Dean RHP	.811	1934	30–7
3	Chris Carpenter RHP	.810	2009	17–4
	Ted Wilks RHP	.810	1944	17–4
4	Chris Carpenter RHP	.808	2005	21–5
5	Harry Brecheen LHP	.789	1945	15–4

FUN FACT: Johnny Allen RHP (Indians) is #1 in MLB with a .938 winning percentage in 1937, he was 15 and 1.

Pitchers: Opponent's Batting Average (OBA or BAA) – Single-Season Leaders

#1	Bob Gibson RHP	.184	1968
#2	Fred Beebe RHP	.193	1908
#3	Jose DeLeon RHP	.197	1989
#4	Dick Hughes RHP	.203	1967
#5	Bob Gibson RHP	.204	1962
	Mort Cooper RHP	.204	1942

FUN FACT: Pedro Martinez (Red Sox) is #1 in MLB for lowest opponent's batting average in a single season with .167 in 2000; Nolan Ryan (Rangers, Astros etc.) is the #1 career leader with .204.

PITCHERS/RELIEF: SAVES LEADERS

Pitchers/Relief: Saves Leaders – Career

#1	Jason Isringhausen RHP	217
#2	Lee Smith RHP	160
#3	Todd Worrell RHP	129
#4	Bruce Sutter RHP	127
#5	Trevor Rosenthal RHP	110

FUN FACT: The #1 in career saves is Mariano Rivera (Yankees) with 652; Trevor Hoffman (Padres) is #2 with 601; and, Lee Smith (Cubs/Cardinals, etc.) is #3 with 478.

Pitchers/Relief: SAVES Leaders – Single Season

#1	Trevor Rosenthal RHP	48	2015
#2	Jason Isringhausen RHP	47	2004
	Lee Smith RHP	47	1991
#3	Bruce Sutter RHP	45	1984
	Trevor Rosenthal RHP	45	2014
#4	Lee Smith RHP	43	1992
	Lee Smith RHP	43	1993
#5	Jason Motte RHP	42	2012

FUN FACT: The #1 in single season saves is Francisco Rodriguez (Angels) with 62 in 2008; Bobby Thigpen (White Sox) is #2 with 57 in 1990, and John Smoltz (Braves–2002) and Eric Gagne (Dodgers–2003) are tied at #3 with 55.

PITCHING BROTHERS: MOST WINS

Combined Victory Records by 2 Pitchers on the Same Team

#1	**Dizzy & Daffy Dean**	49 Wins	1934	Cardinals
#2	Dizzy & Daffy Dean	47 Wins	1935	Cardinals
#3	Gaylord & Jim Perry	38 Wins	1974	Indians
#4	Gaylord & Jim Perry	33 Wins	1973	Indians
#5	Dizzy & Daffy Dean	29 Wins	1936	Cardinals

Jay Hanna "Dizzy" Dean (1930, 1932–37)

- MLB debut with Cardinals on Sept 28, 1930

- Strikeout leader 1932–35

- Wins leader 1934 and 1935

- NL MVP in 1934

- Four-time All-Star

- Career Stats: .302 ERA, 1,163 strikeouts, 150 wins

- Cardinals broadcaster 1941–46

- Jersey #17 retired

- Elected to HOF (1953)

- St. Louis Cardinals HOF

- Paul Dee "Daffy" Dean (1934–39)

- MLB debut with Cardinals on Apr 18, 1934

- No-hitter in 1934 (rookie year)

- Had 19 wins in 1934 and again in 1935

- 1934 World Series numbers: 18 innings pitcher, 2 wins, 11 strikeouts.

- Played for the Giants (1940–41) and Browns (1943)

FUN FACT: Gaylord Perry (Giants/Indians, etc.) was inducted into the HOF in 1991, and closed off his playing career with the Royals in 1983. His brother, Jim Perry, won the Cy Young Award in 1970 with the Twins, and closed off his career with the Athletics in 1975.

POSTSEASON CARDINALS LEADERS: BATTING AND PITCHING

(See "W" for World Series leaders)

Postseason: Batting Cardinals Leaders

Batting Average:	Pepper Martin	.418 (#3 in MLB)
Games:	Yadier Molina	89
Runs:	Albert Pujols	54
Hits:	Yadier Molina	90

Doubles:	Albert Pujols	18
Triples:	Tim McCarver	3
	Willie McGee	3
Home Runs:	Albert Pujols	18
RBI:	Albert Pujols	52
Total Bases:	Albert Pujols	162
Bases on Balls:	Albert Pujols	52
Stolen Bases:	Lou Brock	14

FUN FACT: The #1 in MLB for highest career postseason batting average (BA) is Bobby Brown (Yankees) with .439 (46 plate appearances). Colby Rasmus (Cardinal in 2009, Astros in 2015) is #2 with .423 (35 plate appearances), and Pepper Martin (above) is #3 (60 plate appearances).

Postseason: Pitching CARDINALS Leaders

- Games:
  - Adam Wainwright — 24
  - Lance Lynn — 24

- Innings Pitched: Chris Carpenter — 108.0

- Wins: Chris Carpenter — 10

- Shutouts:
  - Bob Gibson — 2
  - Wild Bill Hallahan — 2

- Strikeouts: Adam Wainwright — 96

- ERA: Ken Dayley — 0.44

- Saves:
  - Jason Isringhausen — 8
  - Jason Motte — 8

- Fewest Hits/9: Ken Dayley — 2.61

- Fewest Walks/9: Jason Motte — 0.83

FUN FACT: Andy Pettitte (Yankees) has the most wins in postseason history with 19 and a Win–Loss% of .600 (276.2 innings pitched).

is for...

QUOTES

"Whoever said 'it's just a game' has never been to St. Louis" (unknown).

QUOTES: A Variety of Cardinals Quotes

Cards Manager Mike Matheny: "Winning is a tradition, winning is an expectation."

HOF Card Stan Musial: "When a pitcher's throwing a spitball, don't worry and don't complain, just hit the dry side like I do."

Commissioner Ford Frick about Stan Musial: "Here stands baseball's perfect warrior, here stands baseball's perfect knight..."

HOF 2B Rogers Hornsby: "People ask me what I do in winter where there's no baseball. I'll tell you what I do. I stare out the window and wait for spring."

HOF Card Tim McCarver about Bob Gibson: "Bob Gibson is the luckiest pitcher in baseball. He is always pitching when the other team doesn't score any runs."

HOF pitcher Bob Gibson: "A great catch (this one was by Curt Flood) is like watching girls go by; the last one you see is always the prettiest."

HOF Card Dizzy Dean about his brother, Paul, throwing a no-hitter in the second game of a double-header when Dizzy threw a two-hitter in the first game: "If I'da known he was gonna throw one, I'da thrown one too."

HOF Card Dizzy Dean on Satchel Paige: "If Satch and I were pitching on the same team, we'd cinch the pennant by July 4th and go fishing until World Series time."

HOF Cards Manager Branch Rickey to Yogi Berra before he signed with the Yankees: "You'll never be a ballplayer. Take my advice, son, and forget about baseball. Get into some other kind of business."

Branch Rickey on running a team: "Luck is the residue of design."

HOF Owner/Manager Bill Veeck on Branch Rickey: "It occurred to me that if I let myself get trapped in a room with Rickey, there was a strong possibility that he would still have (the players I wanted), as well as my promissory note, and I would end up the two guys I never heard of."

HOF Card Enos Slaughter on Branch Rickey: "Mr. Rickey likes baseball players. And he likes money. What he don't like is the two of them getting together." (Roger Kahn)

Mike Shannon (broadcasting from Shea Stadium in New York): "I wish you folks back in St. Louis could see this full moon."

Roger Bresnahan: "No woman can tell me how to play a ball game!" – said to the female owner of the Cardinals, Helene Robison Britton, by then-Cards manager Bresnahan, who was fired by her at the end of the season (63–90 record).

Jack Buck (broadcaster): "Go crazy, folks, go crazy."

FUN FACT: St Louis treasure, ex-player/current broadcaster Mike Shannon is the quote king of the Cardinals; everyone seems to have a favorite "shannonism." Check on-line for some compilations of great quotes like this one about a base stealer: "Sometimes when you feel the urge, you've just gotta go" (6/17/1998). Or just stay tuned to Cards games for new gems!

QUALITY STARTS (QS):

A QS is when a starter completes at least six innings while allowing no more than three earned runs. There are a lot of questions about the value of this statistic (pitchers can have a QS and lose the game, etc.), but some statistics point to teams winning 68% of QS games.

QUALITY STARTS (QS): Cardinals Single-Season Leaders (% of Starts)

#1	**Bob Gibson RHP**	32 (94%)	1968
#2	Mort Cooper RHP	28 (80%)	1942
#3	Chris Carpenter RHP	27 (82%)	2005
#4	John Lackey RHP	26 (79%)	2015
	Adam Wainwright RHP	26 (76%)	2013
	Danny Cox	26 (74%)	1964
#5	Adam Wainwright RHP	25 (78%)	2014
	Bob Gibson RHP	25 (69%)	1964
	Mort Cooper RHP	25 (76%)	1944
	Chris Carpenter RHP	25 (71%)	2010
	Adam Wainwright RHP	25 (74%)	2009

FUN FACT: The QS statistic was invented by Philadelphia Inquirer sportswriter John Lowe in 1985. Wilbur Wood is #1 in single-season QS with 37 in 1971; tied with 36 at #2 are Bob Feller (Indians–1946) and Sandy Koufax (Dodgers–1966).

QUALITY STARTS (QS): Longest Consecutive QS Streaks in MLB History 1913–2016

#1	**BOB GIBSON**	26 QS	1967–68 (Cardinals)
#2	Eddie Cicotte	25 QS	1916–17 (White Sox)
#3	Jake Arrieta	24 QS	2015–16 (Cubs)
	Walter Johnson	24 QS	1914–15 (Senators)
#4	**CHRIS CARPENTER**	22 QS	2005 (Cardinals)
#5	Johan Santana	21 QS	2004 (Twins)
	Greg Maddux	21 QS	1997–98 (Braves)
	Dwight Gooden	21 QS	1984–85 (Mets)
	Pedro Martinez	21 QS	1999–2000 (Red Sox)
	Lon Warneke	21 QS	1933 (Cubs)

FUN FACT: During Bob Gibson's 26-game QS streak, he threw 8 shutouts. In a stretch from June 6 to July 25 that year, he pitched 10 games, completed all 10, won all 10, 8 games were shutouts, and the other 2 he allowed only one run (ERA was 0.20). Chris Carpenter went 17–2 during his 22 QS streak, with a 1.66 era.

QUALITY STARTS (QS): Pitchers with 94% QS of 30+ Total Starts – Single-Season

Bob Gibson	32 of 34	94%	1968 (Cardinals)
Dwight Gooden	33 of 35	94%	1985 (Mets)
Zach Greinke	30 of 32	94%	2015 (Dodgers)

FUN FACT: Some people prefer "True" or "High" QS as a metric: the starter completes seven innings and allows no more than two earned runs. The career #1 in that category is Bob Gibson with 245 of 482 for 50.8% (his standard QS career total is 328 of 482 for 68%).

RBI (Runs Batted In)

RBI: Leaders – Career

#1	**Stan Musial OF/1B**	1,951 (#6 MLB)	
#2	Albert Pujols 1B	1,329	
#3	Enos Slaughter OF	1,149	
#4	Jim Bottomley 1B	1,105	
#5	Rogers Hornsby 2B	1,072	

RBI: Leaders – Single Season

#1	**Joe Medwick LF**	154	(1937) (NL #1)
#2	Rogers Hornsby 2B	152	(1922) (NL #1)
#3	Mark McGwire 1B	147	(1998) (NL #2)
#4	Mark McGwire 1B	147	(1999) (NL #1)
#5	Rogers Hornsby 2B	143	(1925) (NL #1)

FUN FACT: Hack Wilson CF (Cubs) is #1 for single-season RBI with 191 in 1930; this is one those records considered unlikely to be broken. The most recent player to get close was Manny Ramirez OF (Indians) with 165 in 1999 (#14), and Sammy Sosa OF (Cubs) had 160 in 2001 (#21). For career RBI, Alex Rodriguez (IF–Yankees) is close to the top at #3 with 2,086, after #1 Hank Aaron (OF–Braves) with 2,297, and Babe Ruth (OF–Yankees) with 2,214.

RBI: Most Game-Winning RBI (1980–Present):

Rank	Player	Game-Winning RBIs
1	Albert Pujols 1B	204
2	Ray Lankford CF	102
3	Matt Holliday LF	93
4	Jim Edmonds CF	87
5	Willie McGee OF	85
6	Ozzie Smith SS	83

FUN FACT: Keith Hernandez 1B (Mets) had the most game-winning RBI in one season with 24 in 1985; Mark McGwire 1B (Athletics) had 14 in his rookie season.

RECORDS: MLB

Records: Some of the MLB Records Held by Cardinals

- World Series/Most Strikeouts in a game: Bob Gibson 17 K's on October 2, 1968.

- Most RBI in one game: 12, a record held by two Cardinals:

- "Sunny" Jim Bottomley (1B – HOF 1974) on September 16, 1924 vs. the Dodgers; tied with another St. Louis Cardinal

- Mark Whiten (OF) who hit 4 home runs on September 7, 1993 vs. the Reds driving in 12 runs.

- Most Grand Slams in one inning: Fernando Tatis (3B) hit 2 on April 23, 1999.

- Most RBI in one inning: Fernando Tatis (3B) with 8 on April 23, 1999 (see above).

- Last NL Winner of a Triple Crown: Joe Medwick in 1937 with .374 batting average, 31 home runs and 154 RBI.

- Most Triple Crown Winners: 3 – Rogers Hornsby twice (1922 and 1925), Joe Medwick (1937)

- Catcher with 100 Walks, 100 Runs, and 100 RBI in one season: Darrell Porter is one of two, sharing the list with HOF Tiger Mickey Cochrane.

- Highest Batting Average/Season (since 1920): Rogers Hornsby (2B) – .424 (1924)

- Most Shutouts/Single Season (since 1920): Bob Gibson – 13 (1968)

- Defensive WAR Career Leader (since 1974): Ozzie Smith – 43.4

ROOKIE REDBIRDS

ROOKIE OF THE YEAR (ROY) Awards – Cardinals

Slash line: batting average(BA)/on base percentage(OBP)/slugging percent(SLG)

1954	**Wally Moon OF:** 144 Games, .304/.371/.433
1955	**Bill Virdon CF:** 144 games, .281/.322/.433
1974	**Bake McBride OF:** 150 games, .309/.369/.394
1985	**Vince Coleman LF:** 151 games, .267/.320/.335
1986	**Todd Worrell RHP:** 9–10 (36 saves), 2.08 ERA, 73 strikeouts
2001	**Albert Pujols 1B:** 161 games, .329/.403/610

FUN FACT: Jackie Robinson (Dodgers) was the first Rookie of the Year in 1947. Only two players have been named Rookie of the Year and MVP in the same year (both American League): Fred Lynn CF of the Red Sox (1975) and Ichiro Suzuki RF of the Mariners (2001).

MORE FUN FACTS ON THE ROOKIES – Where did they go?

Bill Virdon was traded to the Pirates in 1956, won a Gold Glove in 1962 and then became a coach and manager. Bake "Shake 'n Bake" McBride was an All-Star in 1976, was traded to the Phillies in 1977; he had a career batting average of .299, and returned to coach in the Cardinals system after retirement. Wally Moon replaced Enos Slaughter in the O; unpopular with fans, who chanted, "We want Slaughter" in his first time up. So Moon hit a home run, first at-bat—against the Cubs! He was traded to the Dodgers in 1959. For Worrell and Coleman, check "Where Are They Now" section under "W." You know where Pujols is.

ROOKIE MLB/NL RECORDS HELD BY CARDINALS

MLB Rookie Records: BATTING

Batting Average:	George Watkins	.373 (1930)
Slugging Percentage:	George Watkins	.621 (1930)
Stolen Bases:	Vince Coleman	110 (1965)

NL Rookie Records: BATTING

Runs Batted In:	Albert Pujols	130 (2001)

NL Rookie Records: PITCHING

Saves:	Todd Worrell	36 (1986)

FUN FACT: George Watkins (OF) played in the majors from 1930 to 1936 (Cardinals 1930–33), and never again hit at his NL league record rookie level of .373 in 1930. Vince Coleman was with the Cardinals from 1985–90; his rookie record of 110 steals ranks third for single season after Rickey Henderson's 130 in 1982 and Cardinals Lou Brock's 118 in 1974.

RELIEF PITCHERS – CARDINALS AWARDS

Winners Of The Rolaids Relief Man Award (1976–2012)

Based on statistical performance (highest point score based on relief wins/losses, saves and blown saves)

(Replaced by the Trevor Hoffman award in 2014)

1981	Bruce Sutter	80 points (HOF)
1982	Bruce Sutter	82 points (HOF)
1984	Bruce Sutter	93 points (HOF)
1986	Todd Worrell	80 points
1991	Lee Smith	135 points
1992	Lee Smith	103 points
1995	Tom Henke	104 points

FUN FACT: Mariano Rivera RHP (Yankees) and Dan Quisenberry RHP (Royals/Cardinals) both won this award five times. The winners for the new Trevor Hoffman NL Award so far have been Craig Krimbel RHP (Atlanta Braves) in 2014 and Mark Melancon RHP (Pirates) in 2015.

is for...

SCHOENDIENST, ALBERT FRED ("RED") — HOF 1989

Schoendienst Career Highlights

- Signed by the Cardinals in 1942, Red was MVP the next year in the International League (Rochester Red Wings).

- Served in the Army 1944–45.

- Back with the Cardinals in 1945 (debut 4/17/45 at age 22); in his rookie year that season, led the league in stolen bases with 26.

- 1956 set an NL record with a fielding percentage of .9934.

- A switch-hitter with career batting average of .289 (1945–63).

- 10-time All-Star (1946, 1948–55, 1957).

- As a manager, held a .522 winning percentage in 14 seasons.

- Wore a Major League uniform as player, coach, and manager, for seven decades.

- As the Cardinals manager, led the team to two NL Pennants (1967 and 1968), plus a World Series championship in 1967.

FUN FACT: Red comes from Germantown, Illinois, about 40 miles east of downtown St. Louis. His father was a coal miner, and luckily the Cardinals scout who first looked at him (and passed him over), changed his mind and drove to Red's home to sign him for $75 per month.

SWITCH-HITTERS: NOTABLE CARDINALS

Whitey Herzog's 1985 Cardinals had five switch-hitters in their starting lineup, plus one switch-hitting pitcher, on the roster. They went 101–61 that year and lost to Kansas City in the World Series. Willie McGee said that Whitey liked switch-hitters because he got two players for one (with 5 you get 10 players, etc.).

Switch-Hitters: Herzog 1985

Willie McGee CF

Ozzie Smith SS

Terry Pendelton 3B

Tom Herr 2B

Vince Coleman LF

Joaquin Andujar P

Switch-Hitters: The 1934 World Champions

Frankie Frisch 2B

Ripper Collins 1B

Jack Rothrock OF

Tex Carleton P

Other Notable Cardinals Switch-Hitters:

Red Schoendienst 2B

Ted Simmons C

Lance Berkman 1B

Abraham Nunez 3B

Cesar Ozturis SS

Carlos Beltran OF

Rafael Furcal SS

Dick Schofield SS

Kid Nichols P

FUN FACT: Ted Simmons is considered the best switch-hitting catcher of all time. Red Schoendienst is high up on the all-time list of switch-hitters, as is Lance Berkman, but the number one overall is Yankee legend Mickey Mantle. The speedy Cool "Papa" Bell was maybe the greatest switch-hitter of the Negro Leagues.

SALARIES – CARDINALS

Salaries: Survey of Highest Cardinals Salaries in Select Years – Plus Highest that Year in MLB

(Note: Information sources on salaries seem to disagree but I thought the numbers were interesting nonetheless; consider them "approximate" at best. Cardinals salary info is from baseball-almanac.com and highest MLB salary is from the SABR.com article by Michael Haupert.)

Rogers Hornsby (2B)   **$33,333**   **1925 & 1926**

First year with Cards in 1915: $1,200

Highest salary in MLB 1925/6: Babe Ruth – $52,000

Grover Alexander (P)   **$17,500**   **1927 & 1928**

First year with Cards in 1926

Highest salary in MLB in 1927/28: Babe Ruth – $70,000

Frankie Frisch (2B)   **$18,500**   **1934**

(Joe Medwick made $5,000 in 1934, Pepper Martin $9,000)

Highest salary in MLB 1934: Babe Ruth – $35,000

Daffy Dean (P)	$10,000	1936

First year with Cards in 1934: $5,000

Highest salary in MLB 1936: Mickey Cochrane – $36,000

Dizzy Dean (P)	$25,400	1937

First year with Cards in 1930: $2,500

Highest salary in MLB 1937: Babe Ruth – $80,000

Leo Durocher (SS)	$10,000	1937

First year with Cards in 1933: not available ($6,000 in 1936)

Highest salary in MLB 1937: Babe Ruth – $80,000

Joe Medwick (RF)	$20,000	1938

First year with Cards in 1932: $3,750

Highest salary in MLB 1938: Lou Gehrig – $39,000

Johnny Mize (1B)	$15,000	1940

First year with Cards 1936: not available

Highest salary in MLB 1940: Hank Greenberg – $35,000

Enos Slaughter (RF) $25,000 1950

First year with Cards in 1938: $2,400

Highest salary in MLB 1950: Joe DiMaggio – $100,000

Red Schoendienst (2B) $45,000 1954 & 1955

First year with Cards in 1945: $4,800

Highest salary in MLB in 1954/55: Ted Williams – $85,000

Stan Musial (OF/1B) $100,000 1958 & 1959

First year with Cards in 1941: $1,800

Highest salary in MLB 1941: Ted Williams – $135,000+

Ken Boyer (3B) $70,000 1962–64

First year with Cards in 1955: not available

Highest salary in MLB 1962–64: Mickey Mantle/Willie Mays – $90,000
(1962) and $105,000 (1963/64)

Steve Carlton (P) $40,000 1971

First year with Cards in 1965: $4,500

Highest salary in MLB 1971: Carl Yastrzemski – $167,000

Bob Gibson (P) $175,000 1975

First year with Cards in 1959: not available (1964 – $30,000)

Highest salary in MLB 1975: Hank Aaron – $240,000

Lou Brock (LF) $185,000 1976

First year with Cards in 1964: $20,000

Highest salary in MLB 1976: Hank Aaron – $240,000

Ted Simmons (C) $216,000   1977

First year with Cards in 1968: not available

Highest salary in MLB 1977: Mike Schmidt – $560,000

Ozzie Smith (SS) $3,500,000   1996

First year with Cards in 1982: $450,000

Highest salary in MLB 1996: Cecil Fielder – $9,237,500

Chris Carpenter (P) $15,840,971   2010

First year with Cards in 2004: $500,000

Highest salary in MLB 2010: Alex Rodriguez – $33,000,000

Albert Pujols (1B) $14,508,395   2011

First year with Cards in 2001: $200,000

Highest salary in MLB 2011: Alex Rodriguez – $32,000,000

Yadier Molina (C) $15,000,000   2015

First year with Cards in 2004: $300,000

Highest salary in MLB 2015: Clayton Kershaw (P) – $31,000,000

Adam Wainwright (P) $19,500,000   2016

First year with Cards in 2005: $316,000

Highest salary in MLB 2016: Clayton Kershaw (P) – $34,571,428

FUN FACT: The only St. Louis baseball players to place first overall in salary were in the 19th century: Fred Dunlop made $4,500 in 1886 (Stl/Det) and Paul Cook was at the top with $2,000 in 1891 (Lou/Stl AA). (SABR research by Michael Haupert)

Salaries: MLB Player Historical Milestones

$10,000	Honus Wagner SS	1908 Pirates
	Ty Cobb OF	1913 Tigers
$50,000	Babe Ruth OF	1922 Yankees
$100,000	Joe DiMaggio OF	1945 Yankees
	Hank Greenberg 1B	1947 Pirates
$200,000	Hank Aaron RF	1972 Braves
$500,000	Mike Schmidt 3B	1973 Phillies
$750,000	Catfish Hunter P	1974 Yankees
$1,000,000	Nolan Ryan P	1980 Astros
$5,000,000	Roger Clemens P	1991 Red Sox
	Bobby Bonilla 3B/RF	1992 Mets
$10,000,000	Albert Belle LF	1996 White Sox
$15,000,000	Kevin Brown P	1998 Dodgers
$25,000,000	Alex Rodriguez 2B	2000 Rangers
$32,000,000	Alex Rodriguez 3B	2005 Yankees
$34,000,000	Mike Trout OF	2014 Angels

FUN FACT: In 2016, Zach Greinke [P] became the highest-paid player in MLB history with an average annual value of $34 million-plus (6 years, $206,500,000).

SCORING A GAME: THE OFFICIAL SCORER

Every game—every Cardinals game—has an Official Scorer. They are paid about $150–$200 per game (does not sound like much for such an important job!). The results of the Official Scoring become the box score, official game statistics, and the record of each game.

Scorer: Who are these guys?

Until about 1980, local newspaper writers held those positions but this seemed to be a conflict of interest, for example with the Cardinals reporter scoring the Cardinals game (home advantage, etc.).

Bob Forsch: One of the examples of possible Writer-Scorer conflict cited is one of St. Louis Cardinals pitcher Bob Forsch's no-hitters in 1978. In the eighth inning of that game, the Cardinals 3rd baseman narrowly missed a hard ground ball which the Official Scorer (a local sports writer) judged to be an error, not a hit, thus allowing Forsch to finish up the first no-hitter of the season.

Scorers: Today

Now, the scorers are contractors who can demonstrate the necessary qualifications:

- Knowing MLB "Section 10" rules

- Knowing how to apply the rules

- Knowing how to be aware of the entire field during a play

- Having the integrity to make the correct call

- Having the maturity to make judgment calls, handle questions and challenges

Where does the scorer sit? In the press box.

Do they ever change their minds? Yes, they have up to 24 hours to change a call.

Is there any MLB review? Yes, starting in 2008, an MLB committee was formed to handle challenges, resulting sometimes in overturned scoring decisions. This helped prevent direct arguments between players, managers, and scorers.

SCORING A GAME: BASICS

Get a scorecard and get started – it is not difficult. You need to know a few numbers and abbreviations, and then figure out which system you like (the scoring boxes seem pretty small sometimes). The Cardinals Official 2016 Scorecard is very retro and nice looking; you can order on-line; they also have previous years available. Your other option is to do it with an app on your phone/tablet (the easy way).

Player Number Designations:

1. Pitcher (P)

2. Catcher (C)

3. 1st Baseman (1B)

4. 2nd Baseman (2B)

5. 3rd Baseman (3B)

6. Shortstop (SS)

7. Left Fielder (LF)

8. Center Fielder (CF)

9. Right Fielder (RF)

Classic Double Play (SS to 2B to 1B): **6—4—3**

Hitter grounds to 3B, who throws to 1B: **5—3**

Hitter flies out to LF: **F7**

Some Symbols:

K   Strikeout (backwards K is Strikeout Looking)

BB   Walk

FC   Fielder's Choice

HP   Hit by Pitch

E   Error (with the number of the player, E4 for error by 2B)

For more details and help, check out MLB.com, "Baseball Basics: How to Keep Score," or books like "The Joy of Keeping Score" by Paul Dickson.

#	PLAYER	POS.
6	Stan Musial	3
2	Red Schoendienst	4

FUN FACT: Henry Chadwick (1824–1908), English-born American sportswriter, baseball statistician, and historian, is usually credited with formulating the first scoring system in 1859 documenting runs, hits, put-outs, assists, and errors for the Brooklyn Excelsiors Club. He used "K" for pitchers' strikeouts. Baseball-almanac.com also provides these items:

- The first known scorecard appeared in 1845 for the Knickerbocker Club.

- WW" was a unique scoring notation used by former Yankee-great Phil Rizzuto when scoring as an announcer: "wasn't watching" (an error?).

- President Dwight D. Eisenhower scored every game he attended while in office.

is for...

Total Bases (TB)

TB: the number of bases a player has gained with hits: 1 for a single, 2 for a double, 3 for a triple, and 4 for a home run. Walks and advances on bases after the hit do not count.

TB: Total Bases Cardinals Leaders – Career

#1	Stan Musial (OF)	6,134 (#2 in MLB)
#2	Albert Pujols (1B)	3,893
#3	Lou Brock (LF)	3,776
#4	Rogers Hornsby (2B)	3,342
#5	Enos Slaughter (RF)	3,138
#6	Ken Boyer (3B)	3,011
#7	Jim Bottomley (1B)	2,852
#8	Red Schoendienst (2B)	2,657
#9	Ted Simmons (C)	2,626
#10	Ray Lankford (CF)	2,606

FUN FACT: The MLB career leader in TB is Hank Aaron (Braves) with 6,856. Musial is #2 and Willie MAYS (Giants) is #3 with 6,066. Albert Pujols (Cardinals/Angels) is currently #15 overall with a career total of 5,218.

TB: Total Bases Cardinals Leaders – Single Season

Rank	Player	TB	Year
1	Rogers Hornsby (2B)	450	1922 (#2 in MLB)
2	Stan Musial (OF)	429	1948 (#6 in MLB)
3	Joe Medwick (OF)	406	1927
4	Albert Pujols (1B)	394	2003
5	Albert Pujols (1B)	389	2004
6	Mark McGwire (1B)	383	1998
7	Stan Musial (OF)	382	1949
8	Rogers Hornsby (2B)	381	1924
9	Rogers Hornsby (2B)	378	1921
10	Albert Pujols (1B)	374	2009

FUN FACT: The MLB single-season leader in TB is Babe Ruth with 457 in 1921. Hornsby is #2 (1922), and Lou Gehrig is #3 with 447 (1927).

TRIPLE CROWN WINNERS – THREE CARDINALS

Triple Crown: Leader in Home Runs (HR)/Runs Batted In (RBI)/Batting Average (BA). Triple Crowns can be for MLB overall (best case), or for the league (American or National League). In any case, it is a very difficult accomplishment: only 16 players have achieved the Triple Crown in MLB history (10 in the AL, and 6 in the AL).

- **1922: Rogers Hornsby 2B**
  42 HR/152 RBI/.401 AVG (NL Triple Crown)

- **1925: Rogers Hornsby 2B**
  39 HR/143 RBI/.403 AVG (MLB Triple Crown)

- **1937: Joe Medwick LF**
  31 HR/154 RBI/.374 AVG (NL Triple Crown)

FUN FACT: St. Louis has won the most triple crown titles with 4; in addition to Medwick and Hornsby above, Tip O'Neill (LF for the AL Browns), won a Triple Crown in 1887 (14 HR/123 RBI/.435 BA). The only other player to win two triple crowns (like the Cardinals Rogers Hornsby) is Ted Williams (LF–Red Sox) in 1942 and 1947. Medwick's 1937 triple crown was the most recent in NL history. Miguel Cabrera (3B Tigers/AL) won the Triple Crown in 2012. Surprisingly, the Cardinals have never won a pitching triple crown (best in ERA/Wins/Strikeouts).

TEAM STATS: OFFENSE (BEST YEARS)

Team Offense: 1930 Cardinals

1930 dominates team offense numbers historically. Managed by Gabby Street, the Cardinals went 92–62 and lost to the Philadelphia Athletics in the World Series 4–2.

That season every Cardinals player with over 300 at-bats had a batting average over .300; the only time in MLB history:

- Jimmie Wilson C   .318
- Jim Bottomley 1B   .304 (HOF)
- Frankie Frisch 2B   .346 (HOF)
- Charlie Gelbert SS   .304

- Sparky Adams 3B   .314

- Chick Hafey OF   .336 (HOF)

- Taylor Douthit OF   .303 (HOF)

- George Watkins OF   .373

TEAM STATS: OFFENSE

Category	Rank	Statistic	Year
Batting Average	1	.314	1930
	2	.308	1921
	3	.301	1922
	Lowest Year	.223	1908
Runs	1	999	1930
	2	987	2000
	3	876	2003
	Lowest Year	372	1908
Hits	1	1,732	1930
	2	1,635	1921
	3	1,634	1922
	Lowest Year	936	1981
On Base Plus Slugging % (OPS)	1	.843	1930
	2	.812	2000
	3	.804	2004
	Lowest Year	.554	1908
Runs Batted In (RBI)	1	942	1930
	2	841	2000
	3	827	2003
	Lowest Year	301	1908

TEAM STATS: DEFENSE

Category	Rank	Statistic	Year
Fielding Percentage (FP)	1	.988	2013
	2	.987	2003
	3	.986	2008
		.986	2014
	Worst FP:	.941	1903
Putouts (PO)	1	4,465	1979
	2	4,440	1992
	3	4,437	1968
	Fewest PO:	2,757	1900
Assists (A)	1	2,252	1917
	2	2,044	1907
	3	2,039	1982
	Fewest A:	1,260	1994

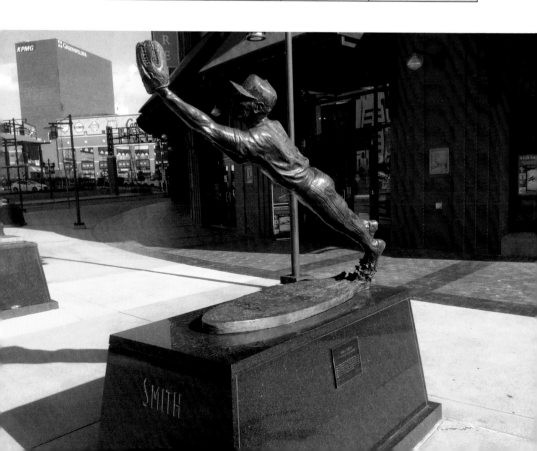

is for...

Unique CARDINALS

Unique History and Facts

- Albert Pujols was drafted 402nd in the 1999 MLB draft.

- Rogers Hornsby did not read books or go to the movies in order to protect his keen eyesight.

- Stan Musial won his last batting title at age 36 in 1957 with a .351 average, while collecting his 3,000th hit.

- Albert Pujols achieved something in each of his first 10 years that no other player has done: he hit at least .300 with 30 homes and 100 RBIs.

- Johnny Mize, in his rookie season (1936), hit .329 with 19 home runs and 93 RBIs.

- Lou Brock set a World Series record for steals (which still stands) with 7 in 1967 and again in 1968.

- Lou Brock, at age 40 in 1979, hit .304 with 21 steals and collected his 3,000th hit; he won Comeback Player of the Year.

- Bob Gibson started his career in sports playing basketball for the Harlem Globetrotters.

- Dizzy Dean, as legend has it, visited the Dodger locker room before a 1933 game and let the players know exactly what pitches he would deliver; he then threw a shutout.

- Dizzy Dean never threw a no-hitter (his brother, Daffy, did), but pitched 23 shutouts in the regular season and 1 in the 1934 World Series.

- Mort Cooper (P) showed off his wins by changing his uniform number to match the victory he was out to get. He started this when he got stuck on 13 wins in 1942, so he changed to number 14 and that worked. He ended up with jersey number 24, earning an NL-best 22 victories and winning MVP honors.

- Harry "The Cat" Brecheen, in seven Cardinals World Series appearances, had a 0.83 ERA in 32.2 innings pitched with 18 strikeouts (1943, 1944, 1946).

"UNBREAKABLE" RECORDS IN MLB (UNLIKELY TO BE BROKEN):

Pitching

Wins/Career: 511	Cy Young (1890–1911)
Wins/Season: 59	Old Hoss Radbourn (1884)
25	Bob Welch (1990) (modern)
Complete Games/Career: 749	Cy Young (1890–1911)
Complete Games/Season: 75	Will White (1879)
48	Jack Chesbro (1904) (modern)
Shutouts/Career: 110	Walter Johnson (1907–27)
No-Hitters/Consecutive: 2	Johnny Vander Meer (1938)
No-Hitters/Career: 7	Nolan Ryan (1966–93)
Strikeouts/Career: 5,714	Nolan Ryan (1996–93)

Saves/Career: 652	Mariano Rivera (1995–2013)
ERA/Season (modern): 1.12	Cardinal Bob Gibson (1968)

Hitting

Hits/Career: 4,256	Pete Rose (1963–86)
200 Hit Seasons/Consecutive: 10	Ichiro Suzuki (2001–10)
Doubles/Career: 792	Tris Speaker (1907–28)
Triples/Career: 309	"Wahoo" Sam Crawford (1899–1916)
Triples/Season: 36	Chief Wilson (1912)
Grand Slams/1 Inning: 2	Cardinal Fernando Tatis (1999)
Batting Average/Career: .366	Ty Cobb (1905)
On Base Percentage/Career: .482	Ted Williams (1939–60)
RBI/Season: 191	Hack Wilson (1930)
Hitting Streak/games: 56	Joe DiMaggio (1941)

One for the RECORD BOOKS

VISIONARY AND INNOVATOR: BRANCH RICKEY

During his 25 years as manager and vice president of the Cardinals (1917–42), Rickey transformed the franchise, and later became famous for breaking the color barrier by signing Jackie Robinson to the Dodgers and for drafting the first Afro-Hispanic superstar, Roberto Clemente, for the Pirates. Here are some of his other innovations:

Farm System: Rickey said that his establishment of the Farm System in MLB was less about inventive genius and more about necessity, trying to compete with less money and a less sophisticated scouting system than his competitors. He took over the Houston Club as a Class A proving ground in 1924, and thus started the minor league system that exists today.

World Series Championships: Rickey laid the foundation for the Cardinals' first four championships in 1926, 1931, 1934, and 1942.

Spring Training: Rickey established the first full-time spring training facility for the Dodgers in Vero Beach, FL.

Helmets and Expansion: Rickey invented the batting helmet, and was an advocate for extending baseball into new markets.

Stats: Rickey pioneered the use of statistical analysis, and promoted the idea that on-base percentage (OBP) was more important than batting average (BA).

HOF: Rickey was elected to the Baseball HOF in 1967.

FUN FACT: Nicknamed "the Mahatma," Rickey was a deeply religious man who refused to participate in Sunday ball games as a player and a manager. Sportswriter Jim Murray said of Rickey, "He could recognize a great player from the window of a moving train."

VITAL STATISTICS: YOUNGEST, OLDEST, HOMEGROWN MISSOURI

Vital Stats: Youngest MVPs in MLB History – Two Cardinals in Top Twenty

(Age: as of final regular season game that year)

STAN MUSIAL 1943:

- #2 Youngest MVP (22 years and 316 days).

- #1 is Johnny Bench of the Reds in 1970 (22 years 298 days old)

- #3 is Bryce Harper of the Nationals in 2015 (22 years 353 days old)

DIZZY DEAN 1934:

- #19 Youngest MVP (24 years 8 months 14 days)

Vital Stats: Cardinals Oldest Players (Mostly Pitchers!)

1.	Gabby Street	C	48 (1931)
2.	Jim Kaat P		44 (1983)
3.	Diomedes Olivo P		44 (1963)

4. Bobby Wallace IF   44 (1918)

5. Jesse Haines P   43 (1937)

Other Cardinals pitchers who ended in their forties: AL Brazle (40), Ellis Kinder (41), Bob McLure (40), Rick Honeycutt (43), and Jesse Orosco (43). Bob Gibson was 39 for his last game. Catcher Walker Cooper and RF Heinie Peitz played until 42.

FUN FACT: The oldest pitcher in MLB history was Satchel Paige (appearing at 59 in 1965). The oldest pitcher who played consecutive MLB seasons was Jack Quinn (50 in 1933, for the Reds). The oldest position player with continuous regular-season play was Julio Franco (49 in 2007 with the Braves).

Vital Stats: Youngest Cardinals (Single Season)

1.	1909	Coonie Blank C	16	(one game)
2.	1924	Ed Clough OF	17	
3.	1959	Tim McCarver C	17	
4.	1924	Ed Clough OF	17	
5.	1999	Rick Ankiel P	19	
	1910	Bunny Hearn P	19	

FUN FACT: The youngest player to start in MLB history is pitcher Joe Nuxhall for the Reds at age 15 on June 10, 1944 against the Cardinals. With the Reds trailing the Cardinals, 13–0, Nuxhall was put into the game. He walked one, and retired two batters before seeing Stan Musial at the plate. Nuxhall came unraveled, allowed five runs and failed to retire another batter. He was sent to the minors and did not pitch again in the majors until 1952, but became an NL All-Star twice and was the NL shutouts leader in 1955.

Vital Stats – MLB Players from MISSOURI:

According to baseball-almanac.com, 293 MLB players were born in St. Louis, and almost 600 were born in Missouri.

HOF – Baseball Hall of Fame from MO:

- Beckley, Jake (1B/Cardinals, etc.): Hannibal (HOF 1971)
- Berra, Yogi (C/Yankees): St Louis (HOF 1972)
- Galvin, Pud (P/OF/Cardinals, etc.): St. Louis (HOF 1965)
- Garagiola, Joe (C/Cardinals, etc.): St. Louis (Frick Award 1991)
- Griffith, Clark (Player/Senators Owner): Clear Creek, (HOF 1946)
- Hubbell, Carl (P/Giants): St. Charles (HOF 1947)
- Stengel, Casey (Manager/Yankees, etc.): Kansas City (HOF 1966)
- Weaver, Earl (Manager/Orioles): St. Louis (HOF 1996)
- Wheat, Zach (LF/Browns): Hamilton (HOF 1959)
- Williams, Dick (Manager/Red Sox, etc.): St. Louis (HOF 2008)

Active Players from MO:

- Arrieta, Jake (P/Cubs): Farmington
- Buehrle, Mark (P/Blue Jays): St. Charles
- Detwiler, Ross (P/Athletics, etc.): St. Louis
- Ellis, A.J. (C/Dodgers): Cape Girardeau
- Freese, David (3B/1B/Cardinals/Pirates): "Honorary" MO (TX)
- Howard, Ryan (1B/Phillies): St. Louis
- Phelps, David (P/Yankees/Marlins): St. Louis
- Robinson, Clint (Utility/Nationals): Jefferson City
- Rosenthal, Trevor (P/Cardinals): Lee's Summit
- Scherzer, Max (P/Nationals/Tigers): Chesterfield
- Van Slyke, Scott (OF/1B/Dodgers): Chesterfield

Notable MLB Players from MO:

- Boyer, Ken (IF/Cardinals, etc.): Liberty (NL MVP 1964)

- Cone, David (P/Yankees, etc.): Kansas City (Cy Young 1994)

- Cooper, Mort (P/Cardinals, etc.): Atherton (NL MVP 1942)

- Cooper, Walker (C/Cardinals, etc.): Atherton
  (only catcher with 10 or more RBIs in a single game/a feat rarer than a perfect game or four-home run game)

- Donaldson, John (P/Negro Leagues–Monarchs, etc.): Glasgow (one of the greatest pitchers of his era with more than 300 wins)

- Holtzman, Ken (P/Cubs, etc.): St. Louis (two no-hitters for Cubs)

- Howard, Elston (C/Yankees): St. Louis (AL MVP 1963)

- King, Silver (P/OF/IF/Browns): St. Louis (AA Wins/ERA champ 1888)

- Knowles, Darald (P/Cardinals, etc.): Brunswick (first pitcher to appear in all seven games of a World Series, in 1973 for the Athletics)

- Oliver, Darren (P/Cardinals, etc.): Kansas City (1st pitcher ever to pitch in an interleague play for Rangers vs. giants; starting Cardinal pitcher when Mark McGwire hit his 61st home run)

- Porter, Darrell (C/Cardinals, etc.): Joplin (First CARD in history to win a NL Championship MVP Award/1982, also won the World Series MVP that year)

- Rogers, Steve (P/Expos): Jefferson City (5-time All-Star, MLB leader in ERA for 1982)

- Robinson, Kerry (OF/Cardinals, etc.): St. Louis (featured in the book Three Nights in August by Buzz Bissinger about a Cardinals–Cubs 3-game series in 2003)

- Shannon, Mike (OF/IF/Cardinals): St. Louis (2-time World Series champion, St. Louis Cardinals HOF, has spent 55 years with the Cardinals organization, and, as a broadcaster, has called games longer than anyone except for Joe Buck)

- Smith, Al (Utility/Indians, etc.): Kirkwood (3-time All-Star, member of 1954 Indians team that won a then-record AL record 111 games)

- Stottlemeyer, Mel (P /Yankees/Coach): Hazelton (5-time All-Star, World Series champion as a coach for the Mets and Yankees)

- Sutcliffe, Rick (P/Dodgers, etc.): Independence (CY young 1984)

VERY VERY OLD-TIME FRANCHISE CARDINALS (1800s)

Jesse "Crab" Burkett LF (HOF): Burkett played for the St. Louis Perfectos (Cardinals) 1899–1901, playing in the majors overall from 1890–1905. He was the 2nd Major League player to bat over .400 twice in 1895 and 96 (first was Ed Delahanty). He holds the record—even today—for the most inside-the-park home runs in MLB history with 55.

Roger Connor 1B (HOF): With the St. Louis Browns (Cardinals) 1894–97, Connor was the home run champion before Babe Ruth (career 138 home runs in an 18-year career). He was a batting champion in 1985, RBI leader in 1889, and finished his career with a .317 batting average.

Silver King P: A native St. Louisan (with a cool name!), King played baseball from 1886–1897 including the St. Louis Browns (Cardinals) from 1887–89. King's best season was for the Browns in 1888: 45 wins, 64 complete games, 258 strikeouts, and a 1.64 ERA; overall for the Browns, he had a .700 win–loss percentage in three years.

Tip O'Neill P/LF: A Canadian, O'Neill played from 1875–92, including some years for the St. Louis Browns (Cardinals) from 1884–89 and 1891. He had a career batting average of .326. In 1884, as a pitcher for the Browns, he went 11–4, with 2.68 ERA and a .733 win–loss percentage. He then switched to outfield, opening a whole new era for himself and winning the triple crown in 1887 with a .435 batting average, 14 home runs, and 123 RBI. His adjusted batting average for 1887 remains the 2nd highest in MLB history.

Slim Sallee LHP: A Cardinal from 1908–1916, Harry "Slim" Sallee ranks #3 in franchise history for ERA with 2.67, #7 in innings pitched (1905.3), and #8 in games started (215) and wins (106, tied with Adam Wainwright). After the Cardinals, Sallee was with the Giants (1916–18), Reds (1919–20), and Giants (1920–21), winning a World Series championship against the "Black Sox" (as a Red) in 1919.

FUN FACT: John McGraw, HOF manager of the New York Giants (1902–32), played one year for the Cardinals in 1900, coming from the Baltimore Orioles. In 99 games at 3rd base, McGraw batted .344, with an OPS of .921, 115 hits, and 85 walks; his career OBP of .474 is third behind Ted Williams and Babe Ruth.

is for...

WALK-UP SONGS, ORGANISTS, AND CARDINALS MUSIC

Walk-up Song: music played as the batter approaches the plate.

Walk-Up Songs – History

According to Jim Caple's article "How MLB Walk-Up Music Became a Designated Hit" (espn.com, September 4, 2015), the Mariners may have been the first to play songs for every player in 1993. But the team picked the songs, usually trying to match the player. For instance, Mariner Jay Buhner's nickname was "Bone" so they played "Bad to the Bone" by George Thorogood & The Destroyers.

The Oakland Athletics were the first team to play rock music at a Major League ballpark in 1981. Roger Inman was their first baseball disc jockey.

For more information, check on-line; the website mlbplatemusic.com is one of the sites that tracks walk-up music for every team.

FUN FACT: Brave's bad-boy closer and immigrant-basher, John Rocker, made news when Twisted Sister asked that the team stop playing their songs for Rocker's walk-up.

Walk-Up Songs: The Cardinals' First? Lou Brock with Ernie Hays:

Theme from *Shaft*: Former Cardinals organist Ernie Hays said that in the early 70s, Lou Brock requested that the theme song frorn Shaft be played for his trips to the plate.

Walk-Up Songs: A Sample of Cardinals Players

Al Hrabosky P (70s)

"Hungarian Rhapsody No. 2" by Liszt

Mark McGwire 1B (1998)

"Welcome to the Jungle" by Guns 'N Roses in 1998

Scott Rolen 3B (2008)

"Rollin'" by Limp Bizkit in 2008

Albert Pujols 1B (2011)

"Go Buck" by Flame, "Five Seconds" by Canton Jones

David Freese 3B (2011)

"Scatman" by Scatman John

Adam Wainwright P (2016)

"Song of the South" by Alabama

Matt Holliday LF (2016)

"WWE: Crank It UP (Bib Show)" by Jim Johnson

Yadier Molina C (2016)

"Probando Voces 2" by Cosculluela

Jedd Gyorko IF (2016)

"Crazy Town" by Jason Aldean

FUN FACT: Rapper Drake and country music star Jason Aldean are among the most popular for walk-up songs. One study alleged that Rock music had the highest batting average and Alternative-Indie the most home runs. High on the "most memorable" music the walk-ups of two closers: Mariano Rivera (Yankees) with "Enter Sandman" by Metallica and Trevor Hoffman (Padres) with "Hell's Bells" by AC/DC.

Walk-ups and Music: Meet the Cardinals Organists

Audrie Garagiola: The wife of Cardinals Baseball HOF broadcaster (and catcher) Joe Garagiola, Audrie played the organ at Sportsman's Park in the sixties. An article in the Pittsburgh Post Gazette (12/12/69 by Bill Christine) on baseball park organists remembered that sportswriters in the downstairs press box at the 1964 World Series enjoyed yelling "Hey, blondie" to Mrs. Garagiola in her organ booth. She had her own talent for picking songs for players. As Stan Musial circled the bases after a home run, she played "Can't Help Lovin' That Man of Mine," and a Wally Moon homer inspired "How High the Moon?"

Ernie Hays: The organist from 1971–2010, Hays was trained as a classical pianist and hailed from Houston, Missouri. He helped popularize walk-up songs and reliever introduction music in St. Louis. Hays introduced "Here Comes the King," the popular Budweiser jingle played at Cardinals games, which is on occasion accompanied by the popular Clydesdales team circling the stadium (see below and "C" for Clydesdales). He also picked music from the Wizard of Oz for fan-favorite Ozzie Smith.

Dwayne Hilton: The Cardinals' current organist. Hilton took over from Hays in 2011. He studied music at Southwest Missouri State, and then landed at Lacefield Music store in St. Louis. Hilton got his opportunity when the Cardinals came shopping for an organ in 2008, at which time they asked if Hilton would be interested in playing too, helping to support Ernie Hays before his retirement. He plays a Lowery Prestige (A5000) organ.

FUN FACT: More than half of baseball stadiums still feature organ music, but a few—notably the Cubs and Dodgers—make it the primary music throughout the game. Cardinals' organ time during games is about 45 minutes, including pre-game tunes, interactive chants, and clap-along moments during the game, and about 20 minutes of post-game music.

MORE FUN FACTS: According to lowreyforum.com, some funny incidents in MLB include the Phillies' keyboardist playing Peggy Lee's "Is That All There Is?" when a fan streaked across the field in the 70s, and another organist, Wilbur Snapp, being ejected for playing "Three Blind Mice" after a questionable call. In the "Who knew where it started?" category, long-time Yankees organist Eddie Layton is credited with scoring the stadium "Charge" cheer.

"HERE COMES THE KING" – a Cardinals Tradition:

The Budweiser Jingle "Here Comes the King" is played in the 7th inning (or during a rally), and at special times, featuring the Budweiser Clydesdale team making the circuit of Busch Stadium. Former organist Ernie Hays played the advertising jingle for 40 seasons, and it continues on with new organist Dwayne Hilton.

"Here Comes the King" Lyrics:

Here comes the King of Beers, here comes the big Number One.
Budweiser beer, the king is second to none.
Just say Budweiser,
You've said it all.
Here comes the King of Beers so lift your glass let's here the call.

Budweiser beer's the one that's leading the rest,
And beechwood aging makes it beer at its best.
One taste'll tell you,
So loud and clear.
There's only one Budweiser beer
(there's only one Budweiser beer)

When you say Bud there's nothing left you can say.
(When you say Bud!)
When you say Bud, The King is right on his way!
(When you say Bud!)
The King is coming, let's hear the call.
When you say Bud, you've said it all.
When you say Bud, you've said it all!
Ya da da da da da da da da da da
(Here comes The King....!)

FUN FACT: "Here Comes the King" was copyrighted in 1971; the music and lyrics are by Steve Karmen, who wrote six other jingles for Anheuser-Busch. Karmen grew up with Bobby Darin, and played with him in a band in the 1950s. Among other jingles, he wrote "I Love New York."

WHIP (WALKS AND HITS PER INNINGS PITCHED):

WHIP: add the number of walks and hits the pitcher gave up by the number of innings pitched (the lower the number, the better).

WHIP: CARDINALS PITCHERS Single Season

#1	Bob Gibson (RHP)	0.85	1968
#2	John Tudor (LHP)	0.94	1985
#3	Mort Cooper (RHP)	0.99	1942
#4	Kid Nichols (RHP)	1.00	1904
#5	Bugs Raymond (RHP)	1.02	1908
#6	Ed Karger (LHP)	1.03	1907
#7	Bob Gibson (RHP)	1.03	1966
#8	Jose DeLeon (RHP)	1.03	1989
#9	Chris Carpenter (RHP)	1.06	2005
#10	Adam Wainwright (RHP)	1.07	2013

FUN FACT: The single-season MLB leader in WHIP is Pedro Martinez (Red Sox) with 0.737. The career #1 in WHIP is Addie Joss (Cleveland 1902–10) with 0.968; Joss had a career ERA of 1.89 (#2 all-time) and a 160–97 win–loss record.

WHIP: CARDINALS Best Team Seasons (Team ERA)

#1	1968	1.12	(2.49)	NL Pennant
#2	1904	1.17	(2.64)	75–69, 5th place

#3	1942	1.18	(2.55)	World Series Champions
#4	1944	1.19	(2.67)	World Series Champions
	1967	1.19	(3.05)	NL Pennant
	1914	1.19	(2.38)	81–72, 3rd place

FUN FACT: The lowest team WHIP in MLB history belongs to the 1904 Boston team with 1.02 (won the AL pennant); the modern era leader (since 1920) is the 1972 Orioles with 1.10 (no titles that year).

WAR: WINS ABOVE REPLACEMENT

WAR: Measures a player's value by evaluating how many more wins he is worth than a replacement-level player, with adjustments for position and league. Numbers: 8+ is MVP, 5+ is All-Star, and 2+ is starter level; higher number is better

WAR: Cardinals Batters – Single Season (BA: batting average)

#1	**Rogers Hornsby**	**12.5**	**1924**	(BA .424) (#9 in MLB)
#2	Rogers Hornsby	11.2	1921	(BA .397)
#3	Stan Musial	11.1	1948	(BA .376)
#4	Rogers Hornsby	10.8	1925	(BA .403)
#5	Rogers Hornsby	10.6	1922	(BA .401)
#6	Stan Musial	9.9	1943	(BA .357)

FUN FACT: For WAR single-season batting, Babe Ruth (Yankees) is the single-season MLB leader with 15.0 in 1923; Ruth holds 5 of the top 6 positions in that category. In career WAR numbers, Babe Ruth is again #1; Rogers Hornsby and Stan Musial are #9 and #10.

WAR: CARDINALS PITCHERS –
Single Season (ERA: Earned Run Average)

#1	Bob Gibson	9.8	1970	(ERA 3.12) (#9 in MLB)
#2	Bob Gibson	8.8	1969	(ERA 2.18)
#3	Bob Gibson	8.6	1968	(ERA 1.12)
#4	Harry Brecheen	7.9	1948	(ERA 2.24)
#5	Dizzy Dean	6.9	1933	(ERA 3.04)

FUN FACT: Pedro Martinez (Red Sox) is #1 for pitchers with 11.6 in 1999. Roger Clemens ranks #1 in career WAR for pitchers.

WORLD SERIES (WS) – CARDINALS

11 World Championships in 19 World Series appearances, 28 times in post season

WORLD SERIES – 19 Cardinals Appearances (Year – Score – Manager)

(wins in red)

1926	Cards–4, Yankees–3	Rogers Hornsby
1928	Cards–0, Yankees–4	Bill McKechnie
1930	Cards–2, Athletics–2	Gabby Street
1931	Cards–4, Athletics–3	Gabby Street
1934	Cards–4, Tigers–3	Frankie Frisch
1942	Cards–4, Yankees–1	Billy Southworth
1943	Cards–1, Yankees–4	Billy Southworth
1944	Cards–4, Browns–2	Billy Southworth
1946	Cards–4, Red Sox–3	Eddie Dyer

1964	Cards–4, Yankees–3	Johnny Keane
1967	Cards–4, Red Sox–3	Red Schoendienst
1968	Cards–3, Tigers–4	Red Schoendienst
1982	Cards–4, Brewers–3	Whitey Herzog
1985	Cards–3, Royals–4	Whitey Herzog
1987	Cards–3, Twins–4	Whitey Herzog
2004	Cards–0, Red Sox–4	Tony La Russa
2006	Cards–4, Tigers–1	Tony La Russa
2011	Cards–4, Rangers–3	Tony La Russa
2013	Cards–2, Red Sox–4	Mike Matheny

FUN FACT: The Yankees have the most World Series appearances with 40 (27–13 for .675 win percentage). The Giants are second with 20 (8–12 with a .400 win percentage. The Cardinals are third with 19 (11–8 with a .579 win percentage). The Dodgers rank fourth with 18 appearances (6–12 with a .333 win percentage). The only teams with no (zero) World Series appearances are the Washington Nationals (Expos) and the Seattle Mariners.

WORLD SERIES: The Cardinals Most Frequent Opponents

Yankees: 5 times (Cards 3, Yankees 2)

1926 (win), 1928 (loss), 1942 (win), 1943 (loss), and 1968 (win)

Red Sox: 4 times (Cards 2, Red Sox 2)

1946 (win), 1967 (win), 2004 (loss), and 2013 (loss)

Tigers: 3 times (Cards 2, Tigers 1)

1934 (win), 1968 (loss), 2006 (win)

Athletics: 2 times (Cards 1, A's 1)

1930 (loss), 1931 (win)

FUN FACT: The Cardinals may have lost the 2013 World Series to the Red Sox, but they decidedly won the 1st World Series Food Truck Throwdown competition, which was a novel city-to-city competition featuring the best of both in a close showdown. St. Louis' winning food trucks included: Cha Cha Chow, Holy Crepe, Completely Sauced, and M Big Fat Greek Truck. Congrats, St. Louis food trucks!

WORLD SERIES: 11 Championships – Highlights, Scores, and Starting Lineups

1926 World Series: 1ˢᵗ Championship (4–3 win over the Yankees)

In their first World Series appearance, the Cardinals were led by HOF player Rogers Hornsby, player/manager.

Cardinals knuckleballer Jesse Haines threw a complete game shutout in Game 3. Babe Ruth hit three home runs in Game 4 (this was the game where Ruth reportedly promised a sick child that he would hit a home run for him).

Pitcher Grover Cleveland "Pete" Alexander helped win the final two games of the series and Hornsby himself provided the tag to Babe Ruth for the final out, ending Game 7 and giving the Cardinals their first World Series championship.

HOFers: Umpires Bill Klem and Hank O'Day, six Cardinals (Hornsby, Alexander, Jim Bottomley, Chick Hafey, Jesse Haines, Billy Southworth), and seven Yankees (Manager Miller Huggins, Earle Combs, Lou Gehrig, Tony Lazzeri, Herb Pennock, Babe Ruth, Waite Hoyt).

Cardinals Starting Lineup (Game 1):

1. Taylor Douthit CF
2. Billy Southworth RF
3. Rogers Hornsby 2B
4. Jim Bottomley 1B
5. Les Bell 3B
6. Chick Hafey LF
7. Bob O'Farrell C
8. Tommy Thevenow SS
9. Bill Sherdell P

1931 World Series: 2nd Championship (4–3 win over the Athletics)

Spit ball pitcher Burleigh Grimes (grandfathered in on the 1920 ban) won 2 for the Cardinals, and "Wild" Bill Hallahan started and won the other two.

27-year-old rookie Pepper Martin led the team offensively and helped stifle a ninth-inning rally by the Athletics with a running catch.

The Cardinals were managed by Gabby Street (Athletics by Connie Mack).

HOFers: Umpire Bill Klem, five Cardinals (Jim Bottomley, Frankie Frisch, Burleigh Grimes, Chick Hafey, Jesse Haines), and six Athletics (Manager Connie Mack, Mickey Cochrane, Jimmie Foxx, Lefty Grove, Waite Hoyt, Al Simmons).

Cardinals Starting Lineup (Game 1):

1. Andy High 3B
2. Wally Roettger RF

3. Frankie Frisch 2B

4. Jim Bottomley 1B

5. Chick Hafey LF

6. Pepper Martin CF

7. Jimmie Wilson C

8. Charlie Geibert SS

9. Paul Derringer P

1934 World Series: 3rd Championship (4–3 win over the Tigers)

The Cardinals team, nicknamed the "Gashouse Gang," featured Joe "Ducky" Medwick, who batted .379 with 5 RBI (had 106 RBI during the regular season), and the pitching Dean brothers (Dizzy and Daffy), who won 2 games each with a total of 28 strikeouts and an overall 1.43 ERA.

The team was led by HOF player-manager Frankie "The Fordham Flash" Frisch.

HOFers: Bill Klem (umpire), six Cardinals (Frisch, Dizzy Dean, Leo Durocher, Jesse Haines, Joe Medwick, Dazzy Vance), and four Tigers (Mickey Cochrane, Charlie Gehringer, Goose Goslin, Hank Greenberg).

Cardinals Starting Lineup (Game 1 – batting order):

1. Pepper Martin 3B

2. Jack Rothrock RF

3. Frankie Frisch 2B

4. Joe Medwick LF

5. Ripper Collins 1B

6. Bill DeLancey C

7. Ernie Orsatti CF

8. Leo Durocher SS

9. Dizzy Dean P

1942 World Series: 4th Championship (4–1 win over the Yankees)

The Yankees' loss was their first since the Cardinals beat them in 1926; in the meantime, they had won 8 championships. The Cardinals set a franchise record that year with 106 regular season wins.

Every Cardinal that year (except for Harry Gumbert) came up through Branch Rickey's farm system; Rickey was with the Cardinals from 1919–1942 as manager/general manager.

Cardinals pitcher Johnny Beazley won two games, pitching 18 innings with a 2.50 ERA, and Whitey Kurowski (3B) hit the winning 2-run homer in the top of the ninth of Game 5.

HOFers: Umpire Carl Hubbard, three Cardinals (Manager Billy Southworth, Enos Slaughter, and Stan Musial), and six Yankees (Manager Joe McCarthy, Bill Dickey, Joe DiMaggio, Joe Gordon, Phil Rizzuto and Red Ruffing)

Cardinals Starting Lineup (Game 1):

1. Jimmy Brown 2B

2. Terry Moore CF

3. Enos Slaughter RF

4. Stan Musial LF

5. Walker Cooper C

6. Johnny Hopp 1B

7. Whitey Kuroswski 3B

8. Marty Marion SS

9. Mort Cooper P

1944 World Series: 5th Championship (4–2 win over the St. Louis Browns)

This was only the 3rd time in World Series history that both teams shared the same home field—Sportsman's Park (the other two being 1921 and 1922 when the Giants and Yankees played at the Polo Grounds in New York City).

This was the Browns' first and last World Series appearance in their 52-year history.

Cardinals pitchers Max Lanier and Ted Wilkes closed out Game 6.

Stan Musial commented that, even though the Cardinals attracted more fans during the season, during the World Series more seemed to be rooting for the underdog Browns.

The Cardinals that year became the first NL franchise to have three consecutive 100-plus win seasons (106 in 1942, 105 in 1943, and 105 in 1944).

HOFers: Umpire Bill McGowan, and three Cardinals (Manager Billy Southworth, Enos Slaughter, and Stan Musial); there were no future HOFers on the Browns.

Cardinals Starting Lineup (Game 1):

1. Jimmy Hopp CF

2. Ray Sanders 1B

3. Stan Musial RF

4. Walker Cooper C

5. Whitey Kurowski 3B

6. Danny Litwhiler LF

7. Marty Marion SS

8. Emil Verban 2B

9. Mort Cooper P

1946 World Series: 6th Championship (4–3 win over the Red Sox)

In the decisive 7th game, HOFer Enos Slaughter made his famous "Mad Dash" for home from first, on Harry Walker's hit, scoring the winning run after Johnny Pesky made a delayed throw. Cardinals pitcher Harry "The Cat" Brecheen got the final six outs in Game 7.

This was the Red Sox's first World Series appearance since their championship in 1918. After this 1946 series, their next World Series was a loss again to the Cardinals in 1967.

HOFers: two umpires (Cal Hubbard, Al Barlick), three Cardinals (Stan Musial, Red Schoendienst, Enos Slaughter) and three Red Sox (Manager Joe Cronin, Bobby Doerr, Ted Williams).

Cardinals Starting Lineup (Game 1):

1. Red Schoendienst 2B

2. Terry Moore CF

3. Stan Musial 1B

4. Enos Slaughter RF

5. Whitey Kurowski 3B

6. Joe Garagiola C

7. Harry Walker LF

8. Marty Marion SS

9. Howie Pollet P

1964 World Series: 7th Championship
(4–3 win over the Yankees)

Mickey Mantle hit 3 home runs in what was his final World Series, for a record-setting total of 18.

The series featured brother-against-brother match-up of Ken Boyer (Cards) and Clete Boyer (Yankees), who both started at 3B.

Cardinals rookie Tim McCarver (22 years old) went 11-for-23 in the series, batting .478. Bob Gibson won two games (lost 1), with 27 innings pitched, and a 3.00 ERA; he was the series MVP. Yankee pitcher Jim Bouton won two games with a 1.56 series ERA.

During the regular season, the Cards gained Lou Brock in the Brock-for-Ernie-Broglio trade.

HOFers: Two Cardinals (Lou Brock and Bob Gibson), and three Yankees (Manager Yogi Berra, Whitey Ford and Mickey Mantle).

Cardinals Starting Lineup (Game 1):

1. Curt Flood CF
2. Lou Brock LF
3. Dick Groat SS
4. Ken Boyer 3B
5. Bill White 1B
6. Mike Shannon RF
7. Tim McCarver C
8. Dal Maxfill 2B
9. Ray Sadecki P

1967 World Series: 8th Championship (4–3 win over the Red Sox)

The series featured the Cardinals against the "Impossible Dream" Red Sox led by triple crown winner Carl Yastrzemski. The 101-win-Cards included NL MVP winner Orlando "Cha Cha" Cepeda, as well as Roger Maris. It was a re-match of the 1946 World Series which the Cardinals won as well.

With Red Schoendienst at the helm, Bob Gibson (winning his second World Series MVP) was spectacular, giving up only three total runs in three complete games, and adding a home run in Game 7. He tied Christy Mathewson (Giants) by giving up only 14 hits in his three complete WS games.

HOFers: Umpire Al Barlick, five Cardinals (Manager Red Schoendienst, Lou Brock, Steve Carlton, Orlando Cepeda, and Bob Gibson), and two Red Sox (Manager Dick Williams and Carl Yastrzemski)

Cardinals Starting Lineup (Game 1):

1. Lou Brock LF
2. Curt Flood CF
3. Roger Maris RF
4. Orlando Cepeda 1B
5. Tim McCarver C
6. Mike Shannon 3B
7. Julian Javier 2B
8. Dal Maxvill SS
9. Bob Gibson P

1982 World Series: 9th Championship
(4–3 win over the Brewers)

Led by manager Whitey Herzog, the series MVP was catcher Darrell
Porter, who also won the NL MVP that year; he was the first Cardinal to
win both in the same year. A Cardinals fan favorite who always played
"like it was Game 7 of the World Series," Porter delivered key hits,
displayed outstanding defensive skills, and was cited for his handling of
the Cardinals pitching staff.

Bruce Sutter pitched the last two innings of Game 7 to earn his
second save.

Brewers' Paul Molitor and Robin Yount set World Series records:
Molitor had a record 5 hits in Game 1, and Yount was the first to have
two 4-hit games.

HOFers: Three Cardinals (Manager Herzog, Ozzie Smith, and
Sutter), and four Brewers (Rollie Fingers, Paul Molitor, Don Sutton,
and Robin Yount).

Cardinals Starting Lineup (Game 1):

1. Tom Herr 2B
2. Lonnie Smith LF
3. Keith Hernandez 1B
4. George Hendrick RF
5. Gene Tenace DH
6. Darrell Porter C
7. David Green CF
8. Ken Oberkfell 3B
9. Ozzie Smith SS
10. Bob Forsch P

uce st

2006 World Series: 10th Championship (4–1 win over the Tigers)

The Cardinals became the 4th team in history to win the Series in their home stadium's debut season (Busch Stadium III). CARDS Manager Tony La Russa became the second in history to lead teams in both leagues to a championship (his previous was with the Athletics in 1989).

Adam Wainwright got the final three outs in Game 5, replacing Jason Isringhausen, who had season-ending surgery. Wainwright got Brandon Inge to strike out to win the series, the first time since 1988 that the World Series win ended on a strikeout.

The MVP was Cardinals SS David Eckstein, who in the last 3 games went 8 for 22 with 4 RBI; in game 4 he went 5-for-5 with three doubles. Eckstein was later honored with throwing out the first pitch in front of 47,000 fans for Game 6 of the 2011 World Series at Busch Stadium III.

HOFers: Cardinals – Manager Tony La Russa; Tigers – none.

Cardinals Starting Lineup (Game 1):

1. David Eckstein SS
2. Chris Duncan DH
3. Albert Pujols 1B
4. Jim Edmonds CF
5. Scott Rolen 3B
6. Juan Encarcion RF
7. Ronnie Belliard 2B
8. Yadier Molina C
9. So Taguchi LF
10. Anthony Reyes P

2011 World Series: 11th Championship
(4–3 win over the Texas Rangers)

The series was notable for the nail-biter Game 6 with the Rangers one strike away from winning the series, but World Series MVP David Freese saved the day. Freese erased the deficit in the bottom of the 9th with a 2-run triple and then won the game with a walk-off HR in the 11th , sending the series to Game 7 and a Cardinals Championship.

In Game 3, Albert Pujols hit 3 home runs, a World Series accomplishment achieved previously by only Babe Ruth and Reggie Jackson (since then, Pablo Sandoval of the Giants did the same in 2012).

The Rally Squirrel was a fan favorite during the series.

HOFers: Cardinals – Manager Tony La Russa, Rangers – none.

Cardinals Starting Lineup (Game 1):

1. Rafael Furcal SS

2. Jon Jay CF

3. Albert Pujols 1B

4. Matt Holliday LF

5. Lance Berkman RF

6. David Freese 3B

7. Yadier Molina C

8. Nick Punto 2B

9. Chris Carpenter P

is for...

XBH: EXTRA BASE HITS

XBH: a base hit that allows the batter to reach safely at 2nd, 3rd, or home (double, triple, or home run) without an error.

XBH: Single-Season Leaders

#1	Stan Musial OF	103	1948	(#1 in 1948)
#2	Rogers Hornsby 2B	102	1922	(#1 in 1922)
#3	Albert Pujols 1B	99	2004	(#1 in 2004)
#4	Joe Medwick LF	97	1937	
#5	Joe Medwick LF	95	1936	
	Albert Pujols 1B	95	2003	
#6	Jim Bottomley 1B	93	1928	
	Albert Pujols 1B	93	2009	
#7	Stan Musial OF	92	1953	
#8	Mark McGwire 1B	91	1998	

#1	Stan Musial OF/1B	1377	(PA: 12,718) (#3 in MLB)
#2	Albert Pujols 1B	915	(PA: 7,433)
#3	Rogers Hornsby 2B	703	(PA: 6,716)
#4	Lou Brock LF	684	(PA: 9,932)
#5	Enos Slaughter RF	647	(PA: 7,713)
#6	Jim Bottomley 1B	644	(PA: 6,007)
#7:	Ray Lankford CF	619	(PA: 6,290)
#8	Joe Medwick LF	610	(PA: 5,057)
#9	Ken Boyer 3B	585	(PA: 7,050)
#10	Ted Simmons C	541	(PA: 6,450)

FUN FACT: Hank Aaron (Braves) is #1 in MLB for career XBH with 1,477, Barry Bonds (Giants) is #2 with 1,440, and Musial is #3. Babe Ruth (Yankees) holds the single-season record with 119 in 1921

EX-CARDINALS OF NOTE: Where Are They Now?

Joaquin Andujar (P) (1981–85)

*1984 NL Wins Leader and Gold Glove Award, All-Star 1984 and 1985; in 1982 and 1984, Cardinals leader in wins, ERA, shutouts, and strikeouts.

After the Cardinals, he played for the Athletics (1986–87) and returned to the Astros (where he started from1976–81) for his final season in 1988. In 1989, he went 5–0 in the Senior Professional Baseball Association (SPBA). After retiring, Andujar returned to the Dominican Republic and started a trucking business. Sadly, he passed away on September 8, 2015, from diabetes-related health problems.

Rick Ankiel (P 1999–2001, 2004 and OF 2007–09)

*Pitching phenom, first full season (age 20) in 2000, struck out batters at a rate of 9.98 per inning, second in the NL to Randy Johnson (HOF), but started having control problems that postseason. He transitioned to OF in 2005, hitting a home run in his debut.

Since 2009, Ankiel played for the Royals/Braves (2010), the Nationals (2011–12), and the Astros/Mets (2013). He is the first player since BABE Ruth to have at least 10 wins as a pitcher, and 50-plus home runs as a hitter. After retirement in 2014, Ankiel served in 2015 as a "Life Skills Coordinator" for the Nationals, mentoring young players; and, in 2016 signed on with FSM for Cardinals broadcast support.

Vince Coleman (LF 1985–90)

*Rookie season (1985) 110 stolen bases (#3 MLB all-time since 1900), the ONLY player to post 3 consecutive 100-plus stolen bases season (1986–107, 1987–109); 6th on career stolen base list with 752; NL Rookie of the Year–1985, Cardinals All-Star 1988 and 1989.

Coleman played with the Mets (1991–93), Royals (1994–95), Mariners (1995), Reds (1996), and Tigers (1997). He attempted a comeback with the Cardinals in 1998, but ended up with the Memphis Redbirds, where he hit .316 in 20 games but opted to retire in May of that year. In 2015–16, Coleman was working as a base-running instructor for the White Sox.

David Eckstein (SS 2005–07)

*Fan favorite for amazing performance in the 2006 World Series (won the MVP Award), batting .364 with 3 runs, 8 hits, and 4 RBI; Cardinals All-Star 2005 and 2006.

After the Cardinals, Eckstein played for the Blue Jays (2008), Diamondbacks (2008), and Padres (2009–10). He returned to St. Louis to throw out the first pitch at Game 6 of the 2011 World Series in front of 47,000 fans. In 2006, Eckstein partnered with a food company to make his own brand of cereal, "Eckso's!" Since retirement, he and his wife started a company, "Her Universe," producing fashion and accessories for female sci-fi fans. Eckstein also has a personal website, www. davideckstein.com.

Ray Lankford (CF/LF 1990–2001, 2004):

*Replaced Willie McGee in CF (Aug 1990), most home runs at Busch Stadium, five seasons of 20 home runs and 20 stolen bases, All-Star in 1997, fielding percentage .997 in 1996.

Lankford played for the Padres from 2001–02, and returned to the Cardinals to finish off with a pinch-hit home run on October 3, 2004, his final Major League at-bat. He helped celebrate the final season at Busch Stadium II in 200. Lankford has a website www.raylankfor16.com and is available for motivational and corporate speaking engagements.

Darrell Porter (C 1981–85):

*Fan favorite for 1982 postseason (won World Series and NLCS MVP Awards); caught two no-hitters (Jim Colborn in 1977 when he was with the Royals, and Bob Forsch's 2nd no-hitter in 1983); one of few catchers to wear glasses (instead of contacts).

After the Cardinals, Porter played for the Rangers (1986–87), and then retired. Born in Joplin, Missouri, Porter started with the Brewers (1971–76) and the Royals (1977–80), and was an All-Star in 1974, and from 1978–80. He was the 6th catcher in history to reach 100 runs and 100 RBI (1979). Sadly, Porter battled with drug problems, and was found dead in Sugar Creek, Missouri on August 5, 2002.

Ted Simmons (C 1968–80):

*One of the best hitting catchers in MLB history (along with Johnny Bench of the Reds); 6–time Cardinals All-Star with the Cardinals.

Simmons closed out his career with the Braves (1986–88) and ended up with a career fielding percentage of .986. He ranks 2nd in MLB for RBI by catchers with 1,389. In 1992, Simmons was the General Manager for the Pirates, and later was Director of Player Development for the Cardinals. In 2015, Simmons joined the Braves as a scout.

Bill White (1B 1959–65, 1969)

*Cardinals 1964 World Series Champion, collected 7 Gold Glove Awards and was an All-Star 8 times.

In 1989, White was elected President of the National League, the first African-American to reach that level in baseball. And, as a broadcaster covering the Yankees from 1971–88, White was the first African-American to do play-by-play regularly for a Major League team. In 2011, White published a book, Uppity: My Untold Story About the Games People Play.

Todd Worrell (P 1985–89. 1992)

*NL Rookie of the Year in 1986, NL Rolaids Relief Man in 1986, Cardinals All-Star in 1988, NL saves leader in 1986, first relief pitcher to save 30 or more games in his first three full seasons.

Worrell signed as a free agent with the Dodgers in 1993 and retired in 1997. His brother, Tim Worrell, was also an MLB pitcher from 1993–2006. Worrell currently owns the Firesteel Creek Hunting Lodge in Pankinton, South Dakota—check out www.firesteelcreek.com. Since retirement, Todd has also been a coach at Westminster Christian Academy in St. Louis and at the River City Rascals (Frontier League), and volunteers with the St. Louis Fellowship of Christian Athletes (FCA).

EX-CARDINALS: SEVEN LIFETIME CARDINALS

NOTE: INCLUDING WAINWRIGHT AND MOLINA ON THE "LIFETIME" LIST.

#1	Stan Musial OF/1B	22	(1941–44, 1946–63)
#2	Bob Gibson RHP	17	(1959–75)
#3	Yadier Molina C	13+	(2004–present)
	Pepper Martin OF/3B	13	(1928, 1930–40, 1944)
#4	Tom Pagnozzi C	12	(1987–98)
#5	Adam Wainwright RHP	11+	(2005–10, 2012–present)
	Terry Moore CF	11	(1935–42, 1946–48)
#6	Ray Blades OF	10	(1922–28, 1930–32)
	Al Brazle LHP	10	(1943, 1946–54)

FUN FACT: As of 2016, 168 players have spent their entire careers with one franchise, with the Yankees leading the list with 25. The longest of those careers belong to Brooks Robinson (Orioles) and Carl Yastrzemski (Red Sox) with 23 years; Musial, Al Kaline (Tigers), and Mel Ott (Giants) are tied at second with 22 years.

Y is for...

YOU'RE OUT! EJECTIONS:

You're out! – The Never Ejected List: Cardinals on the List of Most Games Played without an Ejection (Never Ejected in their careers!)

MLB Rank	Player	Total Games Played
1	Stan Musial	3,026 games
17	Willie McGee	2,201 games
28	George Hendrick	2,048 games
34	Jim Bottomley	1,991 games
60	Curt Flood	1,759 games

FUN FACT: Ted Williams is on the list at #15 (2,292 games), somewhat surprising given his occasional bad temper (mostly directed at the press). Also in the top 25 are Ken Griffey, Jeff Bagwell, Jimmie Foxx, Willie Stargell, Ernie Banks, and Robin Yount. (Thanks to SABR research.)

You're Out!: Most Ejections by Cardinals Managers

#1	40	Tony La Russa 1996–2011	(16 seasons)
#2	21	Whitey Herzog 1980–90	(11 seasons)
#3	17	Frank Frisch 1933–38	(6 seasons)
#4	15	Joe Torre 1990–95	(6 seasons)
	15	Eddie Stanky 1952–55	(4 seasons)
	15	Roger Bresnahan 1909–12	(4 seasons)

FUN FACT: In 1889, baseball rules changed to permit an umpire to remove a player from a game for an offense; before that, players were fined. The first ejected was Dave Orr of the Columbus Colts (American Association) on May 25, 1889; Orr was upset about a call at 3B. The first NL player was ejected one week later: Buck Ewing (Giants) got it for foul language. And, while Cardinals Manager Johnny Keane did not make the above list, he is one of the few to be ejected from both games of a double header (August 4, 1963).

You're Out!: Cardinals World Series Ejections

- **1934**: Joe Medwick   Fight, removed for protection (Oct 9)

- **1985**: Joaquin Andujar   Argued a ball/strike call (Oct 27)

- **1985**: Whitey Herzog   Argued a ball/strike call (Oct 27)

- **1987**: Danny Cox   Argued a ball/strike call (Oct 25)

FUN FACT: HOFer Hughie Jennings (2B/SS – Tigers) was the first World Series ejection in 1907 (argued a caught stealing call). Former Braves Manager Bobby Cox (who holds the record for most ejections with 161) is the only World Series participant to be thrown out of two games (1992 and 1996). There have been no World Series ejections since 1996.

You're out: MLB Umpires Born in St. Louis

RON KULPA (active)

Kulpa was head-butted by Carl Everett (Red Sox) in 2000 during an argument.

During Game 3 of 2011 World Series, Kulpa made a controversial call saying that Cardinal Matt Holliday was safe at first in a potential double-play situation; the Cardinals went on to win the Series. Kulpa reviewed the tape and later admitted that Holliday should have been called out.

Kulpa was the home plate umpire for Justin Verlander's (Tigers) no-hitter in 2007, and Henderson Alvarez's (Marlins) no-hitter in 2013

GERRY DAVIS (active)

Davis was 2nd Base umpire for Randy Johnson's perfect game (Diamondbacks) in 2004.

September 19, 2008, Davis was on the crew for the first call overturned by instant replay in MLB history (Rays' Carlos Pena home run).

Davis was home plate umpire for last game at Shea Stadium on September 28, 2008.

Davis ejected pitcher Michael Pineda (Yankee) for having pine tar on his neck.

DAVID PHILLIPS (retired)

Phillips was the crew chief during the 1979 Disco Demolition Night at the White Sox's Comiskey Park (one of the most historic bad promotion ideas), ordering the White Sox to forfeit the second game of a scheduled doubleheader.

Phillips ejected Gaylord Perry (Mariners) for an illegal pitch in August 1982.

Phillips removed Albert Belle's (Indians) bat to the umpire's locker room after the White Sox alleged it was corked. Indians pitcher Jason Grimsley (aware that the bat was corked) sneaked into the room to replace it with a different bat… one that unfortunately had another name on it (Paul Sorrento). Belle received a 7–game suspension.

FUN FACT: As of 2016, there are 99 umpires listed on the MLB Roster. There are 10 umpires in the Hall of Fame (HOF). HOF umpire Bill Klem worked the most World Series games as an umpire with 18 between 1908 and 1940.

You're Out!: Interesting UMP Facts!

Umpire History

- 1876: First professional umpire (William McLean)
- 1878: NL pays umps $5 per game, usually 1 ump per game
- 1882: Only ump expelled from a game (Richard Higham – gambling)
- 1885: Chest protectors introduced
- 1903: 1st World Series umps: Hank O'Day & Thomas Connolly
- 1909: 1st time four-umpire system used (World Series)
- 1910: Cubs Player/Manager Frank Chance – 1st person ejected from a World Series game (protesting home run call)
- 1912: Use of 2 umpires became standard (1 behind the plate and 1 in the field)
- 1921: Umps started rubbing balls with Lena Blackburne Magic Mud before each game to remove the gloss (still done today)
- 1933: Umps at first All-Star Game in 1933: Bill Dineen, Bill Klem, Bill McGowan, and Cy Rigler
- 1946: 1st graduate from ump training school reached the majors (BILL McKinley)
- 1947: Current 6-man crew established for World Series
- 1952: 4-man crew for regular season games established
- 1953: 1st ump HOFers: Bill Klem and Thomas Connolly

- 1966: 1st black ump in MLB: Emmett Ashford

- 1974: 1st Hispanic ump in MLB: Armando Rodriguez

- 1998: Harry and Hunter Wendelstedt – first father-son umpires to work together in a game

- 2000: Leagues abolished individual crews to merge into one MLB crew

- 2016: MLB umps earn between $100,000 and $300,000 per year

(see "Umpiring Timeline" on mlb.com)

FUN FACT: Some of the most questionable treatment of umpires came from the legendary John McGraw (aka "Mugsy" and "Little Napoleon") during his time as the "rowdiest member" of the Baltimore Orioles in the 1890s, and as the long-time manager of the New York Giants (1902–32). "He ate gunpowder every morning," complained one umpire, "and washed it down with warm blood." By the way, he is second in managerial wins after Philadelphia Athletics Manager Connie Mack with 2,784.

You're Out!: Want to be an UMPIRE?

MLB BASIC REQUIREMENTS:

- HS diploma or GED

- Reasonable body weight

- 20/20 vision (with/without glasses & contacts)

- Good communication skills

- Quick reflexes and good coordination

- Some athletic ability

- Required preliminary training (i.e. professional umpire school)

- A driving record that makes him or her insurable and able to drive employer-provided transportation

UMPIRE SCHOOL PROGRAM:

- 4–5 weeks basic training

- Minor League Development

- Minor League Advanced Course
- Begin in Rookie or Short-A Minor Leagues
- 7–8 years of Minor League umpiring to be considered at MLB level

UMPIRE SCHOOLS:

- Minor League Baseball Umpire Training Academy – St. Petersburg, FL
- Wendelstedt Umpire School – Ormond Beach, FL

FUN FACT: Starting pay for umpires in the minor leagues, at the lowest level (short-season A), is about $2,000 per month, Class A/high-full season is between $2,000–2,400, Double-A pays about $2,300–$2,700 per month, and Triple-A is $2,300–3,500 per month. (mlb.com)

YEAR OF THE PITCHER 1968: BOB GIBSON

Even though 1968 ended in a World Series loss to the Tigers 4–3, this was an enormous year for the Cardinals team, and especially for Bob Gibson. From June 2 to July 30, Gibson allowed only 2 earned runs in 92 innings. For the regular season, the batting average against Gibson was .184 (OBP of .233). In addition to Gibson winning a Gold Glove, SS Dal Maxvill and OF Curt Flood won as well.

Year of the Pitcher 1968: Bob Gibson Stats

13 shutouts (#1 in MLB)

15 game winning streak

28 complete games in 34 starts

Historic modern record 1.12 ERA (#1 in MLB)

258 Adjusted ERA+ (#1 in MLB)

1.77 Field Independent Pitching (FIP) (#1 in MLB)

268 strikeouts

22–9 win–loss record (.710 %)

WAR: 11.9 (#1 in MLB)

RE24 (Base-out Runs Saved): 65.80 (#1 in MLB)

WPA (Win Probability Added): 8.0 (#1 in MLB)

REW (Base-out Wins Saved): 9.1 (#1 in MLB)

World Series: set a WS record of 17 strikeouts in one game

Year of the Pitcher: Bob Gibson Awards

NL MVP

NL Cy Young Award

NL Gold Glove Award

Year of the Pitcher: CARDINALS Stats in 1968

- 97 wins, 65 losses

- 472 runs allowed – lowest total in MLB history (162 games)

- 30 shutouts

Year of the Pitcher: 1968 Cardinals Opening Day Lineup (by Position)

C	Tim McCarver
1B	Orlando Cepeda
2B	Julian Javier
3B	Mike Shannon
SS	Dal Maxvill
LF	Lou Brock
CF	Curt Flood
RF	Roger Maris
P	Bob Gibson

FUN FACT: The numbers in 1968 resulted in the lowering of the pitcher's mound from 15 to 10 inches, and restored the pre-1963 strike zone:

- 21% of wins were shutouts (339 shutouts in 1,619 games).

- 6.84 was the average number of runs scored per game.

- 31 wins for Denny McLain (Tigers); the last 30-game winner in MLB.

- .301 batting average of the AL batting title winner, Carl Yastrzemski (Red Sox OF), the lowest in history.

- .231 overall MLB batting average that year, the lowest in MLB history

is for...

ZEROES: NO-HITTERS

No-hitter: A game in which the pitcher gives up NO hits while pitching at least nine innings. A pitcher can give up a run through other means (walk, hit-by-pitch, error) and can even get a loss for that game.

Zeroes: No-Hitters – Cardinals Trivia

- *Last no-hitter against the Cardinals in St. Louis:* 1906 by Mal Eason of the Brooklyn Superbas.

- *Last no-hitter by the Cardinals in St. Louis:* by pitcher Bob Forsch on September 26, 1983.

- *No-hitters at Busch Stadium III (since 2006):* None, though Kyle Hendricks (Cubs) came close on September 12, 2016, giving up a home run to Jeremy Hazelbaker in the 9th.

Zeroes: No-Hitters – All Cardinals No-Hitters In Order (date & plate umpire)

1. Jesse Haines RHP   July 17, 1924   Hank O'Day

2. Paul Dean RHP   Sept 21, 1934   Bill Klem

3. Lon Warneke RHP   Aug 30, 1941   Jocko Conlan

4. Ray Washburn RHP   Sept 18, 1968   Bill Jackowski

5. Bob Gibson RHP   Aug 14, 1971   Harry Wendelstedt

6. Bob Forsch RHP   Apr 16, 1978   Lee Weyer

7. Bob Forsch RHP   Sept 26, 1983   Harry Wendelstedt

8. Jose Jimenez RHP   Jun 25, 1999   Bruce Froemming

9. Bud Smith LHP   Sept 3, 2001   Phil Cuzzi

FUN FACT: Bob Forsch, the only Cardinal to pitch two no-hitters, has a brother, Ken Forsch (RHP–Houston), who threw his own no-hitter vs. the Braves on April 7, 1979. They are the only set of brothers in MLB history to achieve this feat. Further on Bob Forsch, he played 15 years for the Cardinals (1974–87, 1988) and had a win–loss record of 163–127 (.562%), and a career ERA of 3.67.

Zeroes: No-Hitters – AGAINST the Cardinals In Order (date & location)

1. Christy Mathewson   Giants   July 15, 1901; Home

2. Mal Eason   Brooklyn   July 20, 1906; Home

3. Horace "Hod" Eller   Reds   May 11, 1919; Away

4. Don Cardwell   Cubs   May 15, 1960; Away

5. Gaylord Perry   Giants   Sept 17, 1968; Away

6.	Tom Seaver	Reds	June 16, 1978; Away
7.	Fernando Valenzuela	Dodgers	June 29, 1990; Away
8.	Johan Santana	Mets	June 1, 2012; Away

FUN FACT: According to baseball-almanac.com, the most "no-hit" teams (victims of no-hitters) are the Phillies and Braves tied at 18; after that are the Dodgers (17), and Giants (16). The Cardinals (NL) have 8 (per above), at 14th on the list (Cubs have 7).

Zeroes: No-Hitters – First Major League Start

3 in MLB History – 2 happened in St. Louis (Browns):

1.	**Ted Breitenstein**	Oct. 4, 1891	Browns vs. Louisville Colonels
2.	**Bob Holloman**	May 6, 1953	Browns vs. Philadelphia Athletics

FUN FACT: Breitenstein played 11 seasons, had three 20-win seasons, and ended his career with the Cardinals in 1901. Holloman went on to play a mediocre eleven seasons and, according to a Bill James formula, was the second least likely pitcher in history to pitch his no-hitter.

Zeroes: No-Hitters (Almost)

Cardinals with No-Hitters Broken Up in the 9th Inning (With Only 1 Hit Total in the 9-Inning Game)

- **Rick Wise:** 6/13/73 vs. Reds
  Joe Morgan hit–9th/1 out

- **Mike Morgan:** 7/3/95 vs. Expos
  Wil Cordero hit–9th/1 out

- **Michael Wacha:** 9/24/13 vs. Nationals
  Ryan Zimmerman hit–9th/2 outs

FUN FACT: Cardinals pitcher Alan Benes had a no-hitter going on 5/6/97 vs. the Braves which was broken up by Michael Tucker with 2 outs in the 9th; the Braves went on to get 7 hits in 13 innings. Since 1961, approximately 50 percent of no-hitters carried into the 9th inning made it through to completion; a no-hitter still alive with two outs has a survival rate of about 80 percent.

ZEROES: SHUTOUTS

Shutout: complete game in which a single pitcher (or team) does not allow the opposing team to score a run.

Zeroes: Shutouts – Career Leaders

#1	56	Bob Gibson RHP (#13 in MLB)
#2	30	Bill Doak RHP
#3	28	Mort Cooper RHP
#4	25	Harry Brecheen LHP
#5	24	Jesse Haines RHP
#6	23	Dizzy Dean RHP

FUN FACT: Walter Johnson (RHP–Senators) is the MLB #1 in career shutouts with 110. Grover Cleveland ("Pete") Alexander (Phillies/Cubs/Cardinals) is #2 with 90, and Christy Mathewson (Giants) is #3 with 79.

Zeroes: Shutouts – Single-Season Leaders

#1	13	Bob Gibson RHP	(1968) (#3 in MLB)
#2	10	Mort Cooper RHP	(1942)
#3	10	John Tudor LHP	(1985)
#4	7	Bill Doak RHP	(1914)
#5	7	Dizzy Dean RHP	(1934)
#6	7	Mort Cooper RHP	(1944)

FUN FACT: For #1 in MLB single-season shutouts, Grover Cleveland ("Pete") Alexander (1916–RHP Phillies) and George Bradley (1876–RHP St. Louis Brown Stockings) are tied with 16; Bob Gibson (above) and Jack Coombs (1910–RHP Athletics) are next with 13 each.

Zeroes/Shutouts: Cardinals World Series Shutouts (In Order)

- 1926   Jesse Haines RHP   Game 3 (4–0) vs. Yankees

- 1930   Bill Hallahan LHP   Game 3 (5–0) vs. Athletics

- 1931   Bill Hallahan LHP   Game 2 (2–0) vs. Athletics

- 1934   Dizzy Dean RHP   Game 7 (11–0) vs. Tigers

- 1946   Harry Brecheen LHP   Game 2 (3–0) vs. Red Sox

- 1967   Bob Gibson RHP   Game 4 (6–0) vs. Red Sox

- 1968   Bob Gibson RHP   Game 1 (4–0) vs. Tigers

- 1985   John Tudor LHP   Game 4 (3–0)   vs. Royals

FUN FACT: Christy Mathewson (Giants) holds the record for career World Series shutouts with 4; three of those took place during the 1905 World Series vs. the Athletics in Games 1, 3, and 5 (Giants won 4–1). The series has the distinction of have shutouts in all 5 games; the other two were by Chief Bender (Giants–Game 2), and Iron Joe McGinnity (Athletics–Game 4).

ZEROES: PERFECT GAMES

Perfect Game/Pitcher: The pitcher lasts a minimum of nine innings in which no opposing player reaches base.

ZEROES: Perfect Games (Almost) – Close Calls

While no Cardinals pitcher has ever thrown a perfect game, there are a few games that came close to perfect:

Shelby Miller: On 5/10/2013, Miller recorded 27 consecutive outs in a game after giving up a single to Eric Young, Jr. (Rockies).

Paul "Daffy" Dean: In his no-hitter on 9/21/1934 vs. the Dodgers, Daffy gave up only one walk to Len Koenecke in the first inning and then retired the next 25 batters in a row. The game was the second in a double header and followed Dizzy Dean's shutout, which was a no-hitter for seven innings before yielding a hit in the 8th inning.

Ed Karger: On 8/11/1907, Karger pitched seven perfect innings against the Boston Braves in the second game of a doubleheader called by prior agreement. This is listed in some places as an "unofficial" 7-inning Perfect Game.

FUN FACT: As of 2016, there have been 23 official perfect games and no pitcher has ever thrown more than one. Seven MLB franchises have never been involved in a perfect game on either side: Cardinals, Pirates, Orioles, Royals, Brewers, Padres, and Rockies. Yankee Don Larsen threw the only perfect World Series game in history in 1956. The most recent perfect game was thrown by Mariner Felix Hernandez on August 15, 2012 at Safeco Field.

About the Author

A native of St. Louis, Ann grew up in Webster Groves, which she has described as "one of the best places ever" to spend a childhood. After three years at Mizzou (short of the desired bachelor's degree), and several summers working on the assembly line at White Rodgers where her dad (Rudy Lambert) worked, she moved to Los Angeles where she landed a job with KSHE's sister station, KWEST. Working for a hard rock radio station in L.A. (with former KSHE D.J. Bob Burch), and then with Westwood One (at that time, a radio syndicator), was a great mid-20s experience.

But, at some point, Ann thought more about finding a "real job"—a career—and somehow that led her to the CIA. Cool job? Living overseas? Adventure? CIA! With that job goal in mind, Ann finished up her degree at UCLA and, after graduation, went right into training with the Agency. She spent 25 years working as an operations officer, serving overseas in some exciting and interesting places. It was a great job, made more enjoyable when teamed up later with her husband, Steve, and son, Mikey.

The baseball roots, of course, came naturally from growing up in St. Louis, an amazing Cardinals town. Ann's mom (Rosemary Lambert) went to Burroughs with Branch Rickey's daughter, and remembers him reading Edgar Allan Poe stories, and going to her first baseball game with them. That same mom went on to teach Joe Buck (now a celebrity himself, but at that time Jack Buck's son) in 1st grade at Rossman School. At age 91, Mom still enjoys going to games! Ann's sister, Lisa Holekamp, used to get straight A tickets to games (Ann never qualified) and another sister, Jane Stickney, ended up living next door to none other than the legendary Stan Musial (proximity is special!). So, there you have Ann's 6-degrees of separation to Cardinals fame.

But, how did Ann get from there to writing baseball books? It is not easy to explain going from casual fan to kind-of-crazy fan. Serving overseas, having a son who played baseball, going to local Minor League games and spring training—these things all contributed. Reading about baseball helped her develop a taste for more books. Knowing more than the guys at work about stats was fun; that might have been the big inspiration.

After retirement from the CIA, Ann wrote a book about the Nationals (*Washington Nationals A to Z*) which was published in July 2016. With the Nationals book under her belt, she decided to take on the Cardinals; obviously a bigger challenge given the history and number of books on the subject. This is the result; Ann hopes you enjoy it!

Go Cardinals!

INDEX

APPENDIX

Most of these numbers are from fangraphs.com – check them out for explanations of the various categories.

HITTERS:

BA (Batting Average):

Number of hits divided by at bats.

.340	Excellent
.325	Great
.300	Above Average
.275	Average
.250	Below Average
.225	Poor
.200	Awful

OBP (On Base Percentage):

Measures how often a batter reaches base for any reason other than a fielding error, fielder's choice, catcher interference, dropped/uncaught third strike or fielder's obstruction.

0.390	Excellent
0.370	Great
0.340	Above Average
0.320	Average
0.310	Below Average
0.300	Poor
0.290	Awful

wOBA (Weighted On-Base Average):

Combines different aspects of hitting, weighing each in proportion to their actual run value; the weights change on a yearly basis.

.400	Excellent
.370	Great
.340	Above Average
.320	Average
.310	Below Average
.300	Poor
.290	Awful

SLG (Slugging Percentage):

Total bases divided by at bats.

.600	Excellent
.550	Great
.450	Above Average
.400	Average
.360	Below Average
.300	Poor
.260	Awful

OPS (On-Base plus Slugging Percentage):

Add OBP and Slugging percentages.

1.000	Excellent
.900	Great
.800	Above Average
.710	Average
.670	Below Average
.600	Poor
.570	Awful

ISO (Isolated Power):

ISO is a measure of hitter's raw power and frequency of extra base hits.

0.250 *Excellent*
0.200 *Great*
0.170 *Above Average*
0.140 *Average*
0.120 *Below Average*
0.100 *Poor*
0.080 *Awful*

WAR (Wins Above Replacement) for Position Players and Pitchers:

Stat measures a player's total value/ contributions to the team (if the player gets injured, and was replaced by a Minor League or low-level bench player, how much value would the team be losing?):

0.1 *Scrub*
1-2 *Role Player*
2-3 *Solid Starter*
3-4 *Good Player*
4-5 *All-Star*
5-6 *Superstar*
6+   *MVP*

wRC & wRC+ (Weighted Runs Created and Weighted Runs Created Plus):

wRC is an estimate of the number of runs created by a player; wRC+ makes adjustments for ballpark and factors in the league average.

wRC	wRC+	
105	160	*Excellent*
90	140	*Great*
75	115	*Above Average*
65	100	*Average*
60	80	*Below Average*
50	75	*Poor*
40	60	*Awful*

wOBA (Weighted On Base Average):

wOBA captures the value of all of a hitter's contributions, using a "linear weights" approach assigning coefficients to every contribution dividing by plate appearances.

.400 *Excellent*
.370 *Great*
.340 *Above Average*
.320 *Average*
.310 *Below Average*
.300 *Poor*
.290 *Awful*

wRAA (Weighted Runs Above Average):

Measures the number of offensive runs a player contributes to their team compared to the average player; zero is league average.

40   *Excellent*
20   *Great*
10   *Above Average*
0   *Average*
-5   *Below Average*
-10 *Poor*
-20 *Awful*

PITCHERS

ERA (Earned Run Average – Starting Pitcher):

The mean of earned runs (those not enabled by an error or passed ball) given up per nine innings pitched.

2.50	Excellent
3.00	Great
3.40	Above Average
3.75	Average
4.00	Below Average
4.30	Poor
4.60	Awful

FIP (Field Independent Pitching):

FIP is an estimate of a pitcher's run prevention independent of their defense performance.

2.90	Excellent
3.20	Great
3.50	Above Average
3.80	Average
4.10	Below Average
4.40	Poor
4.70	Awful

ERA-/FIP-/xFIP- (Earned Run Average Minus, Field Independent Pitching Minus, and Expected Field Independent Pitching):

These are park and league-adjust versions of ERA, FIP and xFIP; it is a "simple way" to tell how well a player performed in relation to league average (league average is set to 100).

70	Excellent
80	Great
90	Above Average
100	Average
110	Below Average
115	Poor
125	Awful

WHIP (Walks and Hits Per Innings Pitched):

WHIP measures how many base runners a pitcher allows (divide walks/hits by IP).

1.00	Excellent
1.10	Great
1.25	Above Average
1.32	Average
1.40	Below Average
1.50	Poor
1.60	Awful

K/9 and K% (Strikeouts Per 9 Innings and Strikeout Percentage):

K/9: # of K times 9 divided by IP. K%: divide # of strikeouts by # of plate appearances.

K/9	K%	
10.0	27%	Excellent
9.0	24%	Great
8.2	22%	Above Average
7.7	20%	Average
7.0	17%	Below Average
6.0	15%	Poor
5.0	13%	Awful

BB/9 and BB% (Walks per 9 Innings and Walk Percentage):

BB/9: # of walks times 9 divided by IP. BB%: divide # of walks by # of plate appearances.

BB/9	BB%	
1.5	4.5%	Excellent
1.9	5.5%	Great